JESUS CHRIST

ON

KILLING

BY

SGT. CHARLIE EIPPER

PRESS

Jimmie,

May you learn an amazing thing about Christ.

Charlie Epps   1 John 5: 11-13

Dedicated to the Lord Jesus Christ, Who gave me the gift and passion to complete this book.
May He receive all the glory.

ACKNOWLEDGEMENTS

- My lovely wife, Yvette, who supported me during the last three years of research, writing, and editing. I love you!
- My sisters, Connie Richardson and Susan Valdez, who financially invested in their little brother during this book endeavor.
- My readers, Mark McMullen (U.S. Army Ranger), Sgt. John Spragins (Wichita Falls Police Department, Wichita Falls, Texas), and Senior Airman Jonathan Wilson (United States Air Force), Who provided encouraging words and invaluable feedback after reading *Jesus Christ on Killing*.
- My writing coach, editor, and sister in Christ, Leah Walker, who dedicated her time to lead me through this project.
- My photographer, Lori Wooster of *Reflections Photography*, who provided outstanding selections for my author photo.
- My mentor, Dr. Tom Rodgers (Lead Pastor at Grace Church, Wichita Falls, Texas), who invested over a decade in equipping me with the tools to critically investigate the Scriptures.

TABLE OF CONTENTS

1

SWAT CALL OUT!

U sing deadly force in the line of duty was the furthest thing from my mind on the evening of January 10, 1999. My wife, Yvette, and I had just left a friend's home where I led one of our church's small group meetings. We had mingled, shared a great meal, and examined the Scriptures together. After enjoying the awesome fellowship with my brothers and sisters in Christ, I left refreshed and charged for the week ahead.

As we drove home I felt the buzz of my assigned Special Weapons And Tactics (SWAT) team pager on my hip. I yanked the device from my belt to see who was calling for me. I immediately recognized the phone number was to the Dispatch section at my police headquarters. This was a SWAT call out and I was being summoned to respond to some high risk situation. Since my SWAT teammates and I had not yet been assigned cell phones, my anticipation grew as we drove mile after mile to reach home where I could finally call for the details.

I had been on the police department for about six years but on the SWAT team for a mere 20 months. I was a young SWAT Officer with only a few operations under my belt. However, although I was still relatively new on the team, I had received additional training to become a qualified sniper/observer. That specialized training would prove absolutely essential during the event that was about to unfold. The names of my SWAT teammates have been changed in the following narrative for their privacy and security.

We finally arrived home and I made contact with the dispatchers via our land line telephone. The information was limited but what details I did receive substantially increased my angst. A suicidal young man had forced his mother and an off-duty police officer out of his house at gun point and then barricaded himself inside the residence. My heart raced while considering the suspect's brazen act of actually pointing a weapon at an officer of the law. It didn't require the experience of a veteran operator to recognize this situation had the potential of going south fast.

I drove to the police station to muster with the rest of the team and gather equipment. Our commander, Lt. Kevin, briefed us as more details were relayed from the scene. We obtained intelligence from the suspect's family that there were multiple firearms in the house including the handgun he pointed at the officer. This barricaded suspect was not only suicidal but also heavily armed. Combined with those facts was the determination he demonstrated by brandishing a weapon when he committed aggravated assault on two people. Lt. Kevin briefed our mission was to set an inner perimeter around the suspect's house to contain him. The negotiators would establish communication in attempt to persuade the young man to come out peacefully.

I could not help but obsess on the suspect's earlier acts while we collected our gear from the cramped and crowded equipment locker. I had noticed we generally would not deploy a sniper team during the few call outs I had participated in involving barricaded suicidal subjects. Yet, the feeling in my gut compelled me to speak up.

I respectfully suggested to Lt. Kevin, "Lt., this guy has already pointed a weapon at an officer. I really think we need to deploy a sniper team on this one."

Lt. Kevin replied, "Ok Charlie, you and Ryan grab your sniper gear and cover the front of the residence!"

Ryan and I had attended sniper school together but he had been on SWAT two years prior to my placement on the team. So, we agreed he would be on the sniper rifle while I acted as the cover sniper.

We drove to the Area of Operation and entered the patrol officers' outer perimeter. We parked our vehicle near the spot selected for the command post several houses down from the suspect's residence. I noticed officers from the Negotiator team had already responded and were working from the command post situated in a garage.

Ryan and I collected our gear from the car and began to move toward the inner perimeter. We immediately recognized that we would need to approach the suspect's house while under the protection of cover. We decided to move down the block behind the houses located on the opposite side of the suspect's residence. We hoped for an easy access such as an alley way since our equipment, including additional sandbags, was a bit cumbersome. However, we discovered no alley was provided so we were required to negotiate several back yard fences to finally reach a good position.

We eventually arrived to our destination which was the back yard of the house on the corner of the block. Out of breath from the trek through the back yards, we knocked on the back glass sliding door to the residence. The home owner appeared and we quickly explained the SWAT situation occurring across the street. We also requested to move through his home for we planned to use his front yard as our sniper position. Without hesitation, he allowed us, while wearing balaclava masks and carrying rifles, to travel through his house to reach our desired point.

We made the front yard flowerbed our sniper nest. Ryan and I were able to lie down in a prone position in the flowerbed with a clear view to the front door of the suspect's house. The distance to the front door was about 60 yards. Ryan was on the Steyr SSG .308 caliber sniper rifle while I covered with the team's Colt Sporter 7.62 caliber semi-automatic rifle.

Our mission was to use our optics to gather intelligence on the house and provide lethal coverage for the Arrest/Assault Team. Approximately one minute after we arrived to the flowerbed, I could see our Arrest/Assault Team moving up to a position west of the objective which was to our right.

Soon afterward, Lt. Kevin said over the radio, "The negotiators have made contact with the suspect and are talking with him now."

This is where the situation quickly escalated. Just seconds after Lt. Kevin's broadcast, the suspect exited the front door into the front yard. Ryan and I could see he was carrying what appeared to be a handgun. It was later determined it was a .357 magnum revolver. The man walked to the middle of the yard and fired one round down into the dirt. The sound of that high velocity handgun round was deafening as it echoed off the closely arranged brick homes.

I announced loudly on the radio, "Shots fired! Shots fired!" "The suspect fired a round into the ground!"

The subject then turned around and walked back into his house. I had been somewhat relieved earlier when contact was made by the negotiators but now my heart was racing.

Ryan made the comment, "This is bad, man!" "I think I might have to kill this guy, Charlie!"

Hearing this from a senior operator caused my anxiety to increase even more. Again, the suspect exited his front door just seconds later and stopped in his front yard. We could see he was still carrying the handgun. Ryan looked down his Schmidt and Bender scope and trained his rifle on the suspect. Ryan said, "I can't see him!" "I can't see him!"

The street light to our right was creating a glare on the scope substantially decreasing the ability to see clearly. The man then raised the handgun and pointed it toward an area across the street to our left. He fired the weapon. Blam! The piercing sound of that magnum round was incredible. I called the commander on the radio saying, "Lt., he just fired another round in the direction of some homes down the street."

Lt Kevin responded, "Charlie, if ya'll feel you need to take the shot, you have the green light."

The male again turned and walked back into his home. The negotiators were pleading with the man to stay in his house. They knew he was placing himself in greater danger while outside firing the weapon. The passion of the police negotiator is to end every situation safely and that means for all involved persons including the suspect. This suspect was drastically reducing the chances of a positive outcome with his violent actions.

It was only seconds later when the suspect exited a third time. He walked to his drive way and faced in a westerly direction. Ryan again said, "I can't see him!"

I had noticed it was a bit difficult to see through my scope as well. However, the cover sniper has to be prepared to take the shot if the sniper misses or is unable to safely fire his weapon. I knew our Arrest/Assault Team was just west of the suspect's position. He raised the handgun pointing it in the direction of my fellow operators.

The weapon went off and a flame of fire blasted out from the barrel burning a lighted image of the suspect in my mind.

The suspect had just discharged a round in the direction of other officers placing them in eminent danger of serious bodily injury or death. I was confident my use of deadly force on the suspect at this point would be in compliance with the contemporary rules on the use of deadly force. However, as a Christian, I had another concern. Would I be justified in the eyes of my Lord Jesus Christ if I were to fire my weapon and kill this man in defense of my teammates?

My following action or inaction would be determined by whether I had reconciled the dilemma beforehand in regards to killing as a believer in Christ. I lowered my head to my rifle and established a good cheek weld on the stock. I gazed down the Simmons scope and searched for the subject. I maneuvered the weapon and took aim at my teammates' aggressor.

2

DECISION OF ACTION

T hirteen years later I spoke with the operator who was the Assault Team Point Man that night, Sgt. Terry. As we recollected the operation together, Terry confided in me by sharing his personal perspective. Terry said, "Charlie, in my entire 23 years as a police officer, I've never been as afraid as I was that night when that guy fired at us." "All I could think was, 'I am sure glad Charlie was there.'"

Of course, I had no idea of the fear Terry was experiencing when the suspect fired that .357 magnum revolver in his direction. However, I was completely aware of the violence being perpetrated upon my fellow teammates.

My ears pinned back in readiness to fight and I rapidly squeezed the trigger on my rifle sending three 7.62 caliber rounds down range on the suspect. At that distance of 55 yards, I could see the young man respond after being hit by the first round which we discovered later had struck his cheek bone. He fell toward the ground in a limp fashion as if his body was folding in the middle. The entire event appeared to move in slow motion as his body finally hit the ground and ceased to move. I quickly yelled over the radio, "The suspect is down!"

The Assault Team Leader led his team across our view to the driveway. They secured the suspect and the rest of the scene including the inside of the house. The team leader ordered over the radio, "We need medical down here, now!"

I could smell the acrid odor of burnt gun powder dispersed from my weapon now lingering in the cold night air. A few seconds later, the same team leader requested for the Detective section and a Crime Scene Unit to respond. It was apparent to Ryan the young man was deceased. As I remained in the prone position, he slowly moved up from the ground, rubbed my head, and walked away toward the downed suspect.

Firing this caliber rifle on the training range would typically require hearing protection. However, I heard only three very low pops. Ryan had reacted by covering his left ear since he was lying down to my right. I had experienced the perceptual distortions known as Auditory Exclusion and Slow-Motion Time. In addition, I had no ear pain from the percussion or sound of the high caliber rounds. This came as no surprise since I had received prior training in recognizing these types of phenomena.

I waited in the sniper nest until being relieved by a patrol officer. I placed my weapon on safe and laid it on the ground. I knew the investigating detectives would process the scene, including our position, with video and photographs of exactly how it was situated. Ryan left the Styer sniper rifle lying on the sandbags he used for support.

Lt. Kevin suddenly said over the radio, "Charlie, you and Ryan come to the command post."

I left my Colt Sporter in the flowerbed and began my walk down the street. I was met at the command post by Lt. Kevin who was accompanied by the Chief of Police and his Deputy Chief. Lt. Kevin asked, "Charlie, is there anything you need?"

My reply indicated exactly of whom I was thinking. I said, "I would like to call my wife."

The Chief of Police moved toward me with his right hand extended and a solemn facial expression. He gently said, "Thank you."

I reached out and shook his hand with a firm grip. My perception was the Chief was non-verbally conveying, "I stand with you."

The post operational procedures began immediately. We drove back to the station to put up equipment and have a team de-briefing. I first called my wife and explained what had happened. I was very surprised how calm she was after hearing I had just killed someone. She was also very encouraging and thought she should call my pastor/mentor, Tom Rodgers. He eventually arrived at the station to minister to me.

Tom and I met shortly in our SWAT office where we prayed thanking God for the team's safety and asked for comfort for the family who had just lost a loved one. I later joined the rest of the team for our team de-brief. It was actually a very short meeting. Lt. Kevin planned to schedule a full team session, including the negotiators, with a professional post-crisis counseling group.

The next day of course began with writing the reports and memorandums covering the details of the incident. The Internal Affairs Lt. took a statement from me for his separate investigation which would later be presented to the Chief of Police. The Crimes Against Persons Detectives worked on completing their investigation to be presented to the District Attorney's Office and eventually to the Wichita County Grand Jury. I will describe in more detail my personal experience with the Grand Jury in Chapter Five.

The responses from my chain of command and the people living in the neighborhood of the shooting scene were nothing but positive. In fact, the deceased man was the son-in-law of a fellow officer and friend. He was able to relay the family's words of understanding and encouragement which meant so much to me. I also received cards and letters from officers, friends, and family indicating their support.

However, there was one aspect of the post shooting follow up that was far from pleasant.

I had been required to submit to a psychiatric examination prior to entering both the Police Academy and the SWAT team. It was also department policy that officers pass another psychiatric examination before returning to duty after being involved in an officer-related shooting. An appointment was eventually scheduled for me to visit the psychiatrist. My session with this particular doctor proved to be very troublesome. I left the office disturbed by his awkward questions that seemed to insinuate it was "abnormal" that I was not feeling guilty, having bad dreams, or expressing a reluctance to use deadly force in the future.

I drove directly to the pastoral offices of my church and met with my mentor, Tom. I explained the encounter I had at the doctor's office and the anxiety I was experiencing. I was confused, shaking, and almost in tears. He calmed my heart by reminding me that the world's view of many matters is frequently inconsistent to ours. Yet, I will always remember the Biblically based statement he made to me that day in his office. He said, "Charlie, I want you to pull that trigger again when the situation calls for it."

As a result, I regained my confidence after hearing such affirmation from my mentor. His clarification helped me to form my own opinion of my meeting with the psychiatrist. I concluded my appointment was comparable to an apple seeking guidance from a fence post on how to process life as an apple. That would be ridiculous, right? Well, it was quite apparent the doctor and I were not "on the same page." He and I had a different view particularly on the life experience of killing. Evidently, we did not share the same "grid."

3

THE GRID

E very person has an established mental grid. The Charlie Eipper definition of a grid is: That filter or perspective people use to categorize individual events of life as good, evil, or amoral, formed as a result of training *from that which they give authority*. In other words, my perspective is formed only by the instruction and the source of that instruction I choose to embrace as authority over my life.

The use of deadly force on another individual is an enormous calling for any person. With that in mind, I had not been negligent in being mentally prepared prior to that evening in the flowerbed. I had formed a mental grid or perspective on the moral status of my duty in regards to using deadly force and killing.

Yet, I didn't enjoy that level of confidence ten years prior to January 10, 1999. I was led to confusion and tension in regards to killing as a Christian just prior to entering the U.S. Army helicopter flight school. I will share more on that challenge in Chapter Ten. However, I did eventually develop a solid grid on killing based upon the teachings from that which I give authority, the Holy Bible.

The Bible is not a manual on killing. On the contrary, its main theme is salvation and life. The divinely inspired writings compiled in the Bible reveal the greatest love story ever known to man. This remarkable love is demonstrated by the Creator of the universe as He executes His rescue of sinful and rebellious man from eternal separation from Himself. God's amazing grace toward man is revealed from Genesis to Revelation and it all points to the Savior, Jesus Christ.

There are many topics addressed in the Bible that are not its main theme. The subject of killing is one of those topics. The Bible does not teach that killing other humans is mandatory for a man or woman to be found acceptable before God or have an eternal relationship with Him. In fact, the only killing required for the salvation of men to be possible was that involving the atoning death of His Son.

So, why is an investigation of the Biblical perspective on killing significant or even relevant to one's life experience? The answer is there are many people in the world whose life or occupation potentially involves the killing of another human being (soldiers, police officers, prosecutors, judges, jurists, and executioners). There are citizens who may have killed or will possibly kill during the act of self-defense.

Some of these same people believe in the God of the Bible and His Son Jesus as their Savior. Because of their faith in Christ, they desire the knowledge to live their lives in a way to honor and please the One who has saved them. It behooves the servant to know what the Master deems righteous and what He deems evil. Since the Scriptures of the Bible contain content either spoken or written by people while under the inspiration of God's Spirit, also known as the Spirit of Christ (2 Timothy 3:16-17; 1 Peter 1:10-12), the Biblical view on any subject is ultimately the perspective of Jesus Christ.

If the Bible is not sought for Jesus' perspective on the topic of killing, Christians are vulnerable to the doctrine of the world. We are bombarded with opinions and concepts that are, at best, unhealthy, or at worst, downright unbiblical. If we engage the worldly ideas without a filter built by the Scriptures, we become susceptible to false teaching and doctrine.

There are many popular media sources in which perspectives on killing are broadcast. One of those sources is the movie industry and it is common for the films created in Hollywood to have characters portraying Christians. The 2010 Sylvester Stallone movie *Rambo* is one of the more recent performances in which characters in the movie are depicted as Christians.

In the movie a group of Christian missionaries persuade the reluctant John Rambo (Sylvester Stallone) to take them by boat up the river from Thailand into Burma to provide support to the Karen tribe's people. While in route, they are overtaken by heavily armed Burmese river pirates. Rambo eventually kills the three pirates to save the team, which included a female missionary, Sarah (Julie Benz), who Rambo feared would be raped and killed.

Rambo is eventually able to bring the missionaries to their desired destination. The leader of the missionary group, Michael Burnett (Paul Schulze), makes an interesting comment to Rambo as Burnett is dismounting the boat. Burnett says, "I know you think what you did was right, but taking a life is never right."

The concern is Michael Burnett is portrayed as a Christian missionary. The possible assumption by the viewer is that Burnett's absolute statement to Rambo on killing is authoritative. Burnett is a missionary so his perspective on killing is surely based upon his investigation of the Scriptures, right?

It is dangerous to rely on assumptions. No opinion or doctrine being taught as a Christian principle should go unchecked to confirm it is developed from the Bible. Even the Apostle Paul was held accountable by the Jews in Berea as he taught them about Christ.

The people "searched the Scriptures daily to find out whether these things were so" (Acts 17:10-11).

Therefore, let's be like the Bereans. No human teaching or doctrine supersedes the Scriptures. The Bible is the authority on any subject on which it specifically teaches. On the topic of final authority of the Scriptures, Bible scholar and theologian Dr. Norman Geisler expressed it this way, "When speaking of its divine authority, the Bible makes it clear that this is a final authority, the court of last appeal in everything it affirms (or implies)." Dr. Geisler adds, "Again, the manner of which Jesus and the New Testament writers use the phrase 'it is written' in the Scriptures manifests their belief that it was the final court of appeal in all disputes on which it speaks."(1)

In other words, one shouldn't rely solely on the statement made by a fictional missionary named Michael Burnett or that of any other man. The Bible is the authority in which upon every Christian should form his perspective of the events of life and whether those events are good, amoral, or evil. So, we will be wise and investigate the Scriptures to discover Jesus Christ's true perspective on killing.

We'll begin by addressing the portion of Scripture commonly quoted to argue Burnett's view on killing. I will share more details of my personal struggle with killing which resulted after encountering folks with similar opinions as Burnett's. I have discovered in my own experiences that the sixth commandment is the most popular Biblical text cited during their attempts to persuade me. Therefore, we'll execute a thorough examination of that commandment found in Exodus 20:13 as we begin to put Michael Burnett's statement to the test.

4

THOU SHALL NOT KILL?

I was a U.S. Army helicopter pilot for three years prior to beginning my law enforcement career. As I mentioned in Chapter Three, I hadn't always enjoyed the same confidence in the morality of killing in the line of duty. I will provide more clarity on the cause of my uncertainty later in Chapter Ten when we discuss killing in war and law enforcement. For now I want to draw our attention to the Scriptural abuse conducted by those who confused me on the topic of killing.

I believe Exodus 20:13 is the most cited passage from the Holy Bible by those who embrace the opinion the Bible teaches all killing is immoral. This verse is sometimes translated and quoted as "thou shall not kill." That translation would definitely lead to the conclusion that all killing is immoral because the word "kill" is vague. In fact, if we remained in the context of the verse alone, one might argue it's even immoral to kill animals and other lower forms of life.

Our quest then is to be good Bible detectives and investigate Exodus 20:13 to see if we can accurately determine the intended meaning of this verse. Is the translation of the verb in this verse as "kill" the best translation? Let's first look into the command's location in relationship to the rest of the Bible. We will be using the *New King James Version Bible* for our examination.

Exodus is the second book in the Bible. It is also located in the section of the Hebrew Scriptures known as the Pentateuch which is comprised of the first five books. The Pentateuch was authored by the Prophet Moses while under the inspiration of God's Spirit. Exodus 20:13 is the sixth commandment located in the Decalogue, commonly known as the Ten Commandments. These "ten commandments" were given to Moses by God for His redeemed national people of Israel. In addition to the Decalogue, there are another 603 additional commands in the Mosaic Law. The primary purpose of the Law was to be a type of moral code for the LORD's people.

The "thou shall not kill" commandment falls in the context of Exodus 20:14 and 15 which are "thou shall not commit adultery" and "thou shall not steal." In other words, Exodus 20:13 was placed in the middle of the "thou shall not" commands. The other characteristic of these commands is their reference to the Israelites' personal relationships amongst themselves. For instance, Exodus 20:12, 16, and 17 were those commanding the honoring of parents, not bearing false witness against their neighbor, and not coveting their neighbor's house, wife, servants, and property. Since all of these commands only refer to the treatment of "people," it's contextually unreasonable to include the killing of animals and insects to the meaning of Exodus 20:13.

These negative type commands are given to Israel because the forbidden behavior violates the character of God Himself. If the action is contrary to God's character, it's considered evil or unrighteous. The importance of ascertaining the intended meaning of Exodus 20:13 is to provide the individual with confidence that they are not committing that act and sinning against Him.

An important element to finding the intended meaning of Exodus 20:13 is the translation of the original Hebrew verb that describes the activity forbidden by God. The Hebrew verb is "thou shall not (Heb. *ratsach*)."(2) The same command was documented again by Moses in the book of Deuteronomy, the second giving of the Law. Moses used the same word, *ratsach*, in Deuteronomy 5:17. (3)

This Hebrew word has been translated to the English word "murder" in some versions of the Bible such as the New American Standard and the New King James versions. Simply by definition, the specificity of the word "murder" drastically reduces the options of interpretation. On the other hand, the broad term "kill" leaves room for several possible understandings.

There are many Hebrew scholars who agree that the best translation for *ratsach* in Exodus 20:13 is indeed the English word "murder." We could rely on the advice of their expert opinion. I propose it's more beneficial if we study the contextual uses of other Hebrew terms related to killing and compare them to the contextual uses of the verb found in Exodus 20:13. The goal of this comparative word study is to determine if there is something "unique" to the contextual uses of *ratsach*. When there are other Hebrew verbs also used in contexts involving killing, why did Moses choose to use this term in this case?

We will execute this comparative study with the aid of biblos. com and the Strong's Hebrew Concordance located within that site. Our hope is to reach a conclusion on whether Moses' use of the word *ratsach* in Exodus 20:13 is best translated to the specific term "murder," defined as intentional criminal or immoral homicide, or will the translation to the general term "kill" be sufficient?

It is interesting Moses didn't use *ratsach* when he wrote about the first murder in the Bible. He used the term (Heb. *harag*). This murder is recorded in Genesis 4:8 when Cain killed his brother Abel. Verse 8 reads:

> 8) Now Cain talked with Abel his brother; and it came to pass, when they were in the field, that Cain rose up against Abel and killed (*harag*) him. (4)

This was clearly murder. Cain killed his brother in anger and jealousy because his offering displeased God while Abel's pleased Him. We also observe the reaction of God Himself in verse 10 when the LORD said to Cain, "The voice of your brother's blood cries out to Me from the ground." The LORD punished Cain by driving him out into the land away from His presence. However, He also made a decree in verse 15 that "whoever kills (*harag*) Cain, vengeance shall be taken on him sevenfold." (5) God was demonstrating His grace upon Cain by protecting him from also being murdered.

Does this mean we should conclude *harag* should automatically be translated "murder" every time we view it in the Scriptures? In fact, this term is utilized in the Hebrew Scriptures 167 times. It is found in other murderous contexts located in 1 Kings 18:13 and Psalm 10:8. However, it's also found in a variety of other contexts including the killing of animals (Leviticus 20:15; Isaiah 22:13) and in battle (Joshua 8:24; 2 Samuel 10:18). It is even used to describe when God destroyed vines with hail (Psalm 78:47) and when He slew famous kings (Psalm 138:17-18).(6) Considering its diverse contextual uses other than that of murder, we can better understand why Moses didn't choose *harag* for Exodus 20:13.

Another common term found in contexts involving killing is the Hebrew word (Heb. *nakah*). This term appears 501 times in the Older Testament. It's also found in Genesis 4:15b:

15b) And the LORD set a mark on Cain, lest anyone finding him should kill (*nakah*) him.(7)

Again, the LORD was preventing the "murder" of Cain. Other translations of the word *nakah* are to strike, smite, and defeat. It is used extensively in contexts of battle and war. It's found in Numbers 14:12 describing how God will smite with pestilence, and in Exodus 3:20 as the LORD struck Egypt. Moses was to strike the rock in Horeb (Exodus 17:6), and when one kills an animal that is the property of another person, the property should be restored (Leviticus 24:18, 24). However, it's utilized in other murderous contexts like Deuteronomy 27:24-25.(8)

The Hebrew word (Heb. *muth*) appears 839 times in the Older Testament. It conveys the concept of "bring about the death" or simply "to die" for men as wells as animals (Genesis 33:13). Genesis 2:17 testifies that the day Adam and Eve would eat the forbidden fruit they "shall surely die." It is found extensively in contexts of capital punishment (Genesis 26:11). However, it is also used in contexts when the LORD may cause the death of certain people (Genesis 18:25).(9) Moses used it again in Genesis 37:18-22 where he revealed the conspiracy by Joseph's brothers to murder Joseph as he approached them in Dothan. Verse 18c reads:

18c) "they conspired against him to kill (*muth*) him."

We find yet an additional Hebrew verb in Joseph's story in Genesis 37:22 when Rueben again is quoted as saying, "Shed no blood, but cast him into this pit which is in the wilderness, and do not lay a hand on him."(10) The Hebrew term translated as "shed" in verse 22 is (Heb. *shaphak*) which appears in the Hebrew Scriptures 115 times. It typically is translated "pour" or "shed." It is utilized in Exodus 4:9 for pouring out water from the Nile River onto the ground, and the pouring of blood from sacrificed animals in Leviticus 4:7,18,25. However, Moses also used this word in murderous contexts such as 1 Kings 2:31. (11)

There are three other Hebrew words used frequently in the context of killing or slaughtering animals in ceremonial sacrifices. These words and the tally of their appearances in the Older Testament are (Heb. *shachat*) at 81 times (12), (Heb. *zabach*) at 134 times (13), and (Heb. *tebach*) at 10 times.(14) Each of these are used in a variety of situations other than the killing of animals, including homicide and murder.

Finally, I would like to mention the Hebrew word (Heb. *chalal*) which is used 93 times in the Older Testament and is translated "kill" or "slain." This word also describes a woman who shouldn't be taken as a wife because she is a whore or profaned in Leviticus 21:7. In addition, it is translated as "fatally wounded" in Judges 9:40. So, like the other words we have seen, *chalal* has a variety of contextual uses in the Scriptures.(15)

My goal was to demonstrate how each of the abovementioned Hebrew verbs is found in a variety of contexts which involve killing, including aforementioned situations in which "murder" would be the proper translation. YYet, Moses chose not to use any of them in Exodus 20:13 or Deuteronomy 5:17. He instead used the word *ratsach*. So, we shall investigate the contextual uses of this word and determine if it is distinguished from the other terms we just studied.

According to Strong's Hebrew Concordance, *ratsach* has 47 occurrences in the Hebrew Scriptures. Its short definition, according to Strong's Concordance, is "manslayer." Strong's Exhaustive Concordance expands its uses to include: "put to death", "kill", "manslayer", "murderer." It continues with the following etymology of this word: "A primitive root; properly, to dash in pieces, i.e. kill (a human being), especially to murder — put to death, kill, (man-) slay(-er), murder(-er)."(16)

After investigating all the contexts in which this word is used, I have discovered it certainly has set itself apart from the other terms we have studied. First, *ratsach* is never used in the context involving the killing of animals such as in ceremonial sacrifices. In fact, it's always found in contexts involving the killing of humans. This term is also "never" used in contexts involving battle, national war, or self defense.

Excluding its occurrences in the Decalogue and other portions of Scripture to describe a person as a murderer or a manslayer, *ratsach* typically functions in contexts involving the killing of humans absent of justifiable cause. Yet, to remain consistent with the principle of our study, we must address two exceptional uses of the word. Fortunately, both occurrences are conveniently located in the same context of Numbers 35.

We will cover Numbers 35 extensively in Chapter Six of this book when we investigate Israel's cities of refuge. But for now, we'll examine the two passages containing the exceptional uses of *ratsach*. The LORD gave Moses the following commands in Numbers 35: 26-27;30a:

> 26) 'But if the manslayer at anytime goes outside the limits of the city of refuge where he fled, 27) 'and the avenger of blood finds him outside the limits of his city of refuge, and the avenger of blood kills (Heb. *ve·ra·tzach*) him, he shall not be guilty of blood.(17)

30a) 'Whoever kills a person, the murderer shall be put to death (Heb. *ha·ro·tze·ach*) on the testimony of witnesses; (18)

Evidently, the intended meaning of the forms of *ratsach* in these situations is not immoral homicide. If he kills the manslayer, the avenger of blood is blameless. It's not deemed a criminal homicide although it specifically involves the intentional killing of a person. Additionally, the killing of the murderer is commanded by God. Therefore, the executioner would be blameless as well. Again, we shall investigate the avenger of blood and this legal process in more detail in Chapter Six.

The two particular uses of *ratsach* in Numbers 35 should have little bearing on our translation of the word in Exodus 20:13. Obviously, these are only two of the word's 47 total occurrences. Our theory of a specific translation of "thou shall not murder" is still reasonable. Therefore, we shouldn't rush to illegitimately transfer the meaning of "all intentional homicide" to the verb in Exodus 20:13.

We just witnessed the importance of examining words in their immediate context. It would be just as illegitimate to transfer the meaning of "unjustified intentional homicide" to the Scripture in Numbers 35. We will discuss in more depth the crucial principle which warns against such transfers of meaning in Chapter Five.

Another important related passage is actually located in the Newer Testament where Jesus recited the sixth commandment while instructing on human relational issues. According to Matthew 5:21, Jesus said:

21) "You have heard that it was said to those of old, 'You shall not murder, and whoever murders will be in danger of the judgment.'

Before we even begin to study the verb "murder" in this passage, we are taught this act is condemnable. Jesus warned of judgment for the violator. Whether this is temporal (present) or eternal judgment is irrelevant. The consequence of judgment naturally conveys that this act is unrighteous or sinful.

The Greek word in Matthew 5:21, φονεύω (*phoneuó*), is translated as "murder" in several English Bible versions, including the *New King James Version*. According to the Strong's Greek Concordance within the site biblos.com, this word occurs twelve times in the Newer Testament. After surveying every context where φονεύω (phoneuó) is used, I found it has much in common with the use of *ratsach* in the Older Testament.

First, all of the contexts involve either a direct quote from the Decalogue or situations of intentional unjustified homicide. For example, an accusation of murder is found in Matthew 23:31-35 where Jesus held the children of Israel accountable for killing the "righteous" prophets. The Apostle James condemned his audience for their murder of "the just" in James 5:6.(19)

The other interesting similarity this Greek term has with *ratsach* is the manner in which it is "not" used. It never falls in contexts involving the killing of animals. It's also never explicitly used to describe killing in the scenarios of capital punishment, battle, war, or self-defense. Much like *ratsach* in the Older Testament, φονεύω(*phoneuó*) is limited to contexts that predominately involve the unjustified intentional killing of humans.

As effective as this comparative word study is, it may not be completely persuasive. Perhaps you remain unconvinced that Exodus 20:13 is directed to one type of killing rather than to all killing in general. To be honest, I agree the results are not absolutely conclusive. I applaud you for your critical analysis. So, in order to compliment the evidence we have gleaned from the word study, I would like to submit the issue of logic into our investigation, particularly the law of non-contradiction.

The law of non-contradiction basically states: "A" cannot equal "Non-A." That is a contradiction. If a conclusion is presented declaring two contradicting points are equal, then we must deem the conclusion illogical. In other words, if Charlie Eipper insists "A" equals "Non-A," his theory must be considered illogical. So, how do we apply this principle to our investigation?

If Exodus 20:13 is translated "thou shall not kill," then we have assumed a "general" intended meaning of the command. This interpretation ultimately means that we believe God is teaching all killing is immoral or sinful. If a search of the rest of the Bible exposes situations where God either commands or permits intentional homicide, the general translation and interpretation is in contradiction. Hence, the opinion that Exodus 20:13 declares all killing is sinful must be deemed illogical and a more specific term such as "murder" must be considered.

Therefore, since the commandment's immediate context does not provide conclusive information, we must broaden our examination to aid in interpreting the intended meaning of *ratsach*. Sometimes this involves investigating the entire paragraph, chapter, or book in which a word or verse is found. Yet, it may require the big picture of the entire Bible to reach our goal.

That is how we will proceed in our investigation. We shall search the entire Bible from Genesis to Revelation to determine which interpretation of Exodus 20:13 is the most logical. Our quick glimpse into Numbers 35 should provide a bit of a clue. Regardless, a complete survey of the Scriptures is prudent for any serious investigator. As a necessary first step, we'll take time in Chapter Five to sharpen our investigative skills. We shall familiarize ourselves with the important concepts of mental culpability and situational context which will prove crucial for this type of examination.

5

MENTAL CULPABILITY

W e tread on dangerous ground when we attempt to assign the meaning to anything out of context. We cannot be confident we have accurately ascertained another person's intended meaning of any word or words, whether written or spoken, when the context is absent. J.P. Louw explains in his book *Semantics of New Testament Greek*: "A word does not have a meaning without a context. It only has possibilities of meaning."(21)

Let's use the word "spring" to illustrate this point. It is simply not possible to ascertain the intended meaning of "spring" without first viewing the surrounding context because there are several possible meanings; for example:

1. The man repaired the *spring* on his car.
2. Kangaroos *spring* along the land.
3. The man planned to *spring* his brother from the jail.

It is impossible to determine the intended meaning of the word "spring" when it stands alone. Once we view or hear the word in a specific context, like the sentences above, then we are able to interpret the intended meaning of the word. We can actually visualize the specific type of spring when we're given contextual clues. Now, attempt to interpret my intended meaning of the word "kill" in the following sentence:

Tom killed Charlie.

It would be proper to assign a basic meaning of "kill" in the context of our study as "causing the death of another human being." However, we are still left with a very vague meaning without more information. Not only are we dependent on a grammatical and situational context, but sometimes we must even understand the "cultural" context. For example, imagine yourself as a citizen of Jerusalem or Rome in the 1st century A. D. and someone made the following comment to you:

The Dallas Cowboys are going to kill the Washington Redskins tonight.

Once it's explained that the Dallas Cowboys and Washington Redskins are rival professional sporting teams, you would be on the way to some clarity. That knowledge would assist you in understanding the intended meaning is not that the Cowboys are going to cause the physical death of the Redskins. Like the 21st century American citizen, you would eventually interpret the statement as: The Cowboys are going to significantly defeat the Redskins in a football game.

Just like the example above, more information is needed in this situation where Tom caused the death of Charlie to determine the intended meaning or use of "kill" in that sentence. The following should help since I added a little more of the context:

> Without provocation, Charlie attacked Tom with a knife
> and Tom killed Charlie with his handgun.

The added information or the situational context was essential for us to determine Tom obviously killed Charlie in self-defense. Would it be accurate to assign the same intended meaning to the word "kill" in the context below?

> Tom broke into Charlie's house in the middle of the night
> and killed Charlie while he was sleeping.

We can easily observe that there are two different intended uses or meanings for the word "kill" in the two examples where Tom killed Charlie. If we choose to assign a meaning to a word without considering the context in which it is found, we commit what is called by James Barr as Illegitimate Totality Transfer. Barr explained this phenomenon as:

"The error that arises, when the "meaning" of a word (understood as the total series of relations in which it is used in the literature) is read into a particular case as its sense and implication there, may be called 'illegitimate totality transfer'." (22)

In other words, we commit this type of error when we illegitimately transfer the same meaning to a word, like the word "kill," every time we see or hear the word regardless of the immediate context in which the word is found. This can cause grave problems in obtaining the accurate interpretation of the immediate message we are investigating. This is the dangerous transfer I spoke of in Chapter Four.

The vulnerability to misinterpret the word "kill" is linked to the inherent vagueness of its basic definition. As a result, we are totally dependent on hearing the rest of the context in order to understand the meaning every time we see or hear the word. It's interesting how our law enforcement and judicial system use a similar vague term. Black's Law Dictionary states, "The legal term for killing a man, whether lawfully or unlawfully, is 'homicide.'" Notice there is just as much ambiguity in the word "homicide." As a result, Black's Law Dictionary further instructs:

> "Unlawful homicide at common law comprises the two crimes of murder and manslaughter. Other forms of unlawful homicide have been created by statute: certain new forms of manslaughter (homicide with diminished responsibility, and suicide pacts), infanticide, and causing death by dangerous driving." Glanville Williams, Textbook of Criminal Law 204 (1978). (23)

In our law enforcement and legal system we are still forced to ask two questions when we come upon the word "homicide." First: Was the homicide lawful or unlawful? This is evidence confirming our contemporary civil law recognizes some homicides are legal or justified. Second: If the homicide is unlawful, what type of criminal homicide has occurred? As a response to this dilemma, our legal system has assigned specific terms like "murder" or "manslaughter" to be used alone or in conjunction with "homicide." The goal is to reduce the potential for misinterpretation and quicker understanding of the type of homicide.

For instance, it should help us in interpreting the statement "Tom killed Charlie" if it instead read, "Tom murdered Charlie." The use of a more specific term "murdered" in place of "killed" assists in understanding, even without the situational context, that this killing was intentional homicide absent of justifiable cause.

As we were instructed before, additional forms of unlawful homicide have been labeled by statute. Each of these forms of criminal homicide has a different title and level of punishment assigned to them. The determination of which form of criminal homicide has occurred is based upon the "mental culpability" of the accused.

Therefore, mental culpability and situational context are indispensable in establishing the moral or legal status of any situation involving the killing of one person by another. Mental culpability is also an inseparable aspect in the prosecution and punishment of specific offenses found in penal codes or codes of law.

The word "culpability" is derived from the root word "culpa." Below are definitions of "culpa," "culpable," and "culpability" found in the Black's Law Dictionary:

Culpa- [Latin]- 1. Roman and civil law. Fault, neglect or negligence; unintentional wrong. 2. Roman law. Conduct that made a party to a contract, or quasi-contract, liable to the other party.(p.406 Black's Law Dictionary Eighth Deluxe Edition)

Culpable- adj. 1. Guilty; blameworthy.

Culpability- n. Blameworthiness; the quality of being culpable. Except in cases of absolute liability, criminal culpability requires a showing that the person acted purposely, knowingly, recklessly, or negligently with respect to each material element of the offense. (24)

Notice the words used in these definitions such as "fault" and "blameworthiness." It's also noted there is a burden of proof that must be reached in order to find a person culpable or blameworthy. In order to prosecute a person for a criminal offense it must be proven that the suspect acted "purposely, knowingly, recklessly, or negligently." Observe also how these four terms flow from the highest level of intent to the lowest. Nevertheless, regardless of the level of intent there is still blame assigned for the commission of criminal activity such as unlawful homicide.

"Criminal homicide" is defined as homicide prohibited and punishable by law, such as murder or manslaughter. It is the act of purposely, knowingly, recklessly, or negligently causing the death of another human being.(25) Since there is criminal homicide that occurs with different culpable mental states, there are titles assigned to distinguish them. For instance, section 19 of the Texas Penal Code assigns specific titles for offenses involving criminal homicide and their required culpable mental states:

Title	**Culpable Mental State**
Capital Murder	Intentionally and knowingly
Murder	Intentionally and knowingly
Manslaughter	Recklessly
Criminally Negligent Homicide	Criminal Negligence

These titles make it more expedient for us to interpret a homicide or killing without the context that was required to form them. The above list of offenses begins with the highest level of intent and ends with the lowest in regards to the required culpable mental state. In addition, each offense above involves a distinctive degree of heinousness as well. Consequently, the punishment for each of these criminal homicides will also differ in its level of severity.(26)

For example, according to the Texas Penal Code, the punishment for Capital Murder is life in prison or the death penalty. The punishment will become less severe, as in years in prison, as we move down the list ending with Criminally Negligent Homicide, which carries a punishment of a minimum of 180 days to no more than two years in a state jail. This indicates that our legal system

41

recognizes that it is unreasonable to consider all situations involving criminal homicide the same in all respects including punishment.

Does this mean that all intentional homicides are considered criminal? No. For example, one of the possible punishments for Capital Murder in the State of Texas is the death penalty. The state's administration of the death penalty is an intentional homicide of the person convicted for a capital offense. However, it is deemed legal rather than criminal.

Another type of justified intentional homicide occurs when deadly force is used by one person on another in certain contexts. The definition of deadly force found in Section 9.01 of the Texas Penal Code reads as follows:

> "Deadly force means force that is intended or known by the actor to cause, or in the manner of its use or intended use is capable of causing, death or serious bodily injury."(27)

Section Nine of the Texas Penal Code continues on to give guidance on the justified uses of force and deadly force. The topics covered are the justified uses of force and deadly force in the protection of persons, the protection of property, for law enforcement, and other special relationships. Section 9.21(c) specifically speaks of the justifiable use of deadly force in situations where the actor reasonably believes the deadly force is specifically required by statute or unless it occurs in the lawful conduct of war.(28)

It's obvious that our human governments have recognized there are different levels of criminal homicide. The type of homicide is determined by the proven mental culpability of the suspect who caused the death of another person. There are specific terms used to help define the type of criminal homicide which are far more beneficial in the interpretation process than vague words like "kill."

As a result, there are also assigned punishments for each category of criminal homicide that differ in severity.

We have also discovered not all intentional homicide is considered criminal and punishable by the law. Therefore, although a specific term is used to describe the homicide, we still must personally investigate the situational context. Only then will we reach an accurate answer in regards to the mental culpability of the actor. If the killing is determined to have been intentional, the situational context will reveal whether the intentional homicide was criminal or justified.

A prime example of implementation of the above principles of situational context and mental culpability involves the investigation of a police officer-related shooting that has resulted in the death of another person. Regardless of how obvious the context or evidence points to a justifiable homicide, the terms "Homicide" or "Justifiable Homicide" will be placed in the title section on the Detective's Prosecution Report and the officer is labeled a suspect. This is because the officer has intentionally caused the death of another person.

The detectives or other assigned authorities will closely investigate the situational context and the evidence with the intent to accurately articulate exactly what happened in a shooting death. Once the authorities are finished with the investigation, the facts of the case are presented before a Grand Jury. The Grand Jury will then reach one of two conclusions. Either an indictment of the officer for criminal homicide will be presented or they will declare the killing as righteous and will hand down a no-bill. The same process would occur for any type of intentional homicide to answer the question of justification, i.e. civilian self-defense.

I explained in Chapter Two the post shooting follow-up procedures I experienced in January, 1999. The department decided that our own Detectives section, with the aid of the District Attorney's Office, would investigate the incident. The original report indicated a homicide had occurred and I was listed as the suspect. After the investigation was complete, the case was presented to the Wichita County Grand Jury by the District Attorney. I was eventually summoned to appear before the jury members.

As I drove to the Wichita County Court House, my mind conjured up several scenarios. Although I was confident of the legality of my actions, I still imagined the possibility of hearing from the jurors, "We have determined to indict you for Murder." Isn't it amazing how we beat ourselves up at times? I thought to myself, "no way!" I was consoled by remembering my confidence was in Christ and His approval of my use of deadly force that night.

I arrived at the court house and started the long trek up to the fourth floor. The Grand Jury room was located up a weird section of stairs in an eerie corner of the building. I finally reached the door and the District Attorney escorted me into the room. I was told to sit in a chair facing the nine-member panel. The jurors were seated behind a semi-circle table that stretched from my left side to my right. As you can imagine, this was intimidating. However, my racing heart and pounding head would soon be calmed.

The Grand Jury Foreman spoke for the group. He started by sharing his personal gratitude for the accomplishment of my duties. As he spoke, I began to think to myself, "Charlie, you're going to be fine." My heart rate slowed and my headache began to fade.

Finally, the Foreman said, "Officer Eipper, we have viewed the evidence of this case and have determined your use of deadly force was justified." He then added, "We thank you for your service." The Foreman stood up and led the group in giving me a standing applause.

After shaking many hands and receiving even a few hugs, I left the building and drove back to the police station. It felt so good to have that event behind me. More importantly, individuals in our legal system gave me more than just affirmation of my use of deadly force and killing. That Grand Jury panel took the time to convey their appreciation as citizens in our community for my service to them. Only another warrior would understand the pride and motivation ignited in my heart after receiving such recognition from those whom I serve and protect.

So, we now have a grasp on how our contemporary and secular legal system has chosen to analyze and label events involving the killing of persons. The next logical step is to investigate the Bible to answer a few questions. For instance, has God decreed for man to demonstrate the same sense of urgency in determining the moral status of any homicide based upon mental culpability? Has He instructed that there are different forms of criminal homicide? Has the LORD instructed that even intentional homicide in certain circumstances may be declared righteous? I am confident we will discover the answers to these questions in the next chapter as we move our investigation to Numbers 35 and explore the LORD's implementation of the Cities of Refuge.

6

THE CITIES OF REFUGE

I magine wandering aimlessly as a stranger in a foreign land for 40 years. The nation Israel did exactly that as they experienced judgment from God for their disobedience. The LORD's national people failed to trust in Him when He commanded them to march into Canaan and take it as their promised land. As a result, He condemned that generation. They would never cross the Jordan and claim their inheritance. The nation wandered in the wilderness for 40 years until that generation died.

In Numbers 34 the great prophet Moses documented the ending of that period of judgment. The children of Israel were back on the eastern edge of the Jordan and on the verge of moving into Canaan to inherit the land. The LORD gave Moses instructions on where their borders would be established and how the land would be divided amongst the tribes of Israel. The LORD's guidance in the next chapter is particularly intriguing in regards to our study on mental culpability and situational context.

In Numbers 35:1-5 the LORD told Moses which cities would be given to the Levite tribe. The LORD then commanded the prophet to appoint six of those cities for a special purpose. Notice the specifics recorded in Numbers 35:6,11-15:

6) "Now among the cities which you will give to the Levites you shall appoint six cities of refuge, to which a manslayer may flee. And to these you shall add forty-two cities.

11) 'Then you shall appoint cities to be cities of refuge for you, that the manslayer who kills any person **accidentally** (emphasis mine) may flee there. 12) 'They shall be cities of refuge for you from the avenger, that the manslayer may not die until he stands before the congregation in judgment. 13) 'And of the cities which you give, you shall have six cities of refuge. 14) 'You shall appoint three cities on this side of the Jordan, and three cities you shall appoint in the land of Canaan, which will be cities of refuge. 15) 'These six cities shall be for refuge for the children of Israel, for the stranger, and for the sojourner among them, that anyone who kills a person accidentally may flee there.

The six cities described in Numbers 35:6 were to be places of refuge or asylum for the person labeled a "manslayer." Numbers 35:11 provides the culpable mental state for this particular offense. These cities were to provide protection to anyone living in the land with the children of Israel who accidentally killed another person. The manslayer would receive shelter from the one whom we will later discover is also known as the "avenger of blood."

The word "accidentally" conveys a mental culpability lower than other levels implied by such words as intent, knowledge, and purpose. Evidently, the LORD held His people to a very strict standard in regards to taking a life. This is evident by the accountability of even the one who accidentally kills another person.

At this point it may seem prudent to review an exhaustive list of definitions of "accidentally" from all of the popular dictionaries, or provide information on the etymology or origin of the word. Yet, as discussed in Chapter 5, it will be more beneficial for us to search the immediate context in order to discern the LORD's intended meaning of this adverb. The ability to view specific actions that supply the basis for this culpable mental state would also be valuable. Fortunately, the LORD did provide example situational contexts in Numbers 35:16-24. We'll first look at Numbers 35:16-21 which provides five example situational contexts describing the actions of the one called a murderer:

> 16) 'But if he strikes him with an iron implement, so that he dies, he is a murderer; the murderer shall be put to death. 17) 'And if he strikes him with a stone in the hand, by which one could die, and he does die, he is a murderer; the murderer shall be put to death.18) 'Or if he strikes him with a wooden hand weapon, by which one could die, and he does die, he is a murderer; the murderer shall be put to death. 19) 'The avenger of blood himself shall put the murderer to death; when he meets him, he shall put him to death. 20) 'If he pushes him out of hatred or, while lying in wait, hurls something at him so that he dies, 21) or in enmity strikes him with his hand so that he dies, the one who struck him shall surely be put to death. He is a murderer. The avenger of blood shall put the murderer to death when he meets him.

It's abundantly clear that these five types of homicides involve the culpable mental states of intent, purpose, and knowledge. Notice also the punishment for the murderer is the same in all five cases, the death penalty. In fact, the LORD assigned the responsibility of executing the murderer to the one called "the avenger of blood." The avenger of blood would be a blood relative, sometimes also translated as "kinsman redeemer," who would dispense capital punishment to the person who is convicted for the murder of their loved one.

The LORD was not commanding or condoning revenge killing. On the contrary, He established this method as a means of exacting His vengeance and wrath on the murderer. It also provided the relatives of the victim with a sense of justice by allowing the "avenger of blood" to be involved in the administration of the death penalty. In Chapter 8, when we research God's instructions to Noah in Genesis 9:5-6, we'll begin to witness God's consistent desire for man to experience justice through participation in capital punishment.

Numbers 35:22 begins with the word "however." This alerts us for coming instruction that differs somewhat or totally from the previous commands for dealing with the killer in verses 16-21. Verses 22-24 read:

> 22) 'However, if he pushes him suddenly without enmity, or throws anything at him without lying in wait, 23) 'or uses a stone, by which a man could die, throwing it at him without seeing him, so that he dies, while he was not his enemy or seeking his harm, 24) 'then the congregation shall judge between the manslayer and the avenger of blood according to theses judgments.

The book of Deuteronomy, the fifth and final book of the Pentateuch, follows the book of Numbers. Deuteronomy 19:4-6 also provides an example situational context which aids in recognizing the culpable mental state of the manslayer:

> 4) "And this is the case of the manslayer who flees there, that he may live: whoever kills his neighbor **unintentionally** (emphasis mine), not having hated him in the past- 5) "as when a man goes into the woods with his neighbor to cut timber, and his hand swings a stroke with the ax to cut down the tree, and the head slips from the

handle and strikes his neighbor so that he dies-he shall flee to one of these cities and live; 6) "lest the avenger of blood, while his anger is hot, pursue the manslayer and overtake him, because the way is long, and kill him, though he was not deserving of death, since he had not hated the victim in time past."

Notice the word "unintentionally" is used to describe the mental state of the manslayer. It's also explicitly clear the manslayer is not deserving of death. The LORD then distinguishes the relative culpable mental state of the murderer from that of the manslayer in Deuteronomy 19:11-13:

11) "But if anyone hates his neighbor, lies in wait for him, rises against him and strikes him mortally, so that he dies, and he flees to one of these cities, 12) "then the elders of his city shall send and bring him from there, and deliver him over to the hand of the avenger of blood, that he may die. 13)"Your eye shall not pity him, but you shall put away the guilt of innocent blood from Israel, that it might go well with you."

Although the English version of the above passages uses the words "accidentally" and "unintentionally" to describe the blame-worthiness of the suspect, the situational contexts also listed above in Numbers 35:22-24 and Deuteronomy 19:4-6 sound very similar to our established contemporary culpable mental states. It appears the manslayer acted recklessly or at least negligently when he killed the victim which would fit the required mental states of our contemporary criminal offenses of manslaughter and criminally negligent homicide.

As a reminder, Moses wrote these Scriptures in Deuteronomy while under the inspiration of the Spirit of Christ. We conclude it's His mandate to distinguish modes of homicide by determining the killer's mental culpability. He also explicitly assigned different punishments for each offense. The murderer was to be delivered to the avenger of blood who would execute him. On the other hand, although the manslayer is not deserving of death, he shall not escape accountability to the judicial system. We'll now view the specific penal sentence for the manslayer as we research God's designed purpose of the cities of refuge in Numbers 35:25-29:

> 25) 'So the congregation shall deliver the manslayer from the hand of the avenger of blood, and the congregation shall return him to the city of refuge where he had fled, and he shall remain there until the death of the high priest who was anointed with the holy oil. 26) 'But if the manslayer at any time goes outside the limits of the city of refuge where he fled, 27) 'and the avenger of blood finds him outside the limits of the city of refuge, and the avenger of blood kills the manslayer, he shall not be guilty of blood, 28) 'because he should have remained in his city of refuge until the death of the high priest. But after the death of the high priest the manslayer may return to the land of his possession. 29) 'And these things shall be a statute of judgment throughout your generations in all your dwellings.

The cities of refuge actually provided two services for those living in the land of Israel. First, they were a place to where they could safely flee from the avenger of blood after they accidentally killed a person. A trial would commence in the city where the offense occurred or the suspect's "land of possession." If the suspect was convicted, the manslayer would be assigned to live in the city of refuge where he had fled. Once the high priest had died, the manslayer could return to the land of his possession.

As a result, the cities of refuge also provided a second service. They functioned as a type of confinement or detention because the manslayer would be sentenced to remain within the borders of the assigned city. The punishment of "city arrest" offered some comfort for the avenger of blood and other loved ones of the victim. They would witness as justice was served by reducing the manslayer's freedom, even for a short time, to travel amongst the land or remain at home with his family and friends.

Although the homicide was unintentional, there still would be mourning and anger in the hearts of the victim's family (Deuteronomy 19:6). The family of the deceased would be delivered from looking upon the manslayer in their land of possession as if the homicide never occurred. Similar to the convicted contemporary offender of manslaughter or criminally negligent homicide, the manslayer was sentenced to a type of imprisonment.

If the manslayer violated the law by leaving the city limits, he became free game. The avenger of blood had the legal authority to execute the fugitive if he caught him outside the city limits prior to the death of the high priest. This would be consistent with the legal principle instructed in Deuteronomy 17:8-13 where the LORD commanded the penalty of death for the one who failed to heed to their assigned legal punishment. For that reason, the avenger of blood shall not be guilty of blood or held liable to any penal punishment for killing the manslayer in this particular context.

Therefore, we have discovered that the astute observation of the immediate situational context is just as necessary to ascertain the Biblical perspective on any recorded intentional homicide. The culpable mental state of the avenger of blood was without a doubt intentional when he executed the convicted murderer and when he killed the fugitive manslayer. Yet, neither of those homicides was considered criminal or immoral. The killing of the murderer by the avenger of blood obviously occurred in the immediate context of capital punishment or the death penalty.

The killing of the fugitive manslayer by the avenger of blood was commanded by God as a justified intentional homicide because the manslayer violated his penal punishment by leaving his assigned city of refuge too early. These were judicial actions taken under the direct order and guidance of the LORD Himself which means these intentional homicides were in accordance to His righteous standard.

In summary, the Scriptures in Numbers and Deuteronomy provide evidence that the LORD has pronounced the necessity of considering the culpable mental state and immediate situational context in regards to determining the moral status of any killing. Additionally, He does not consider all criminal homicide equally condemnable in regards to severity of punishment. The punishments for intentional and unintentional homicide were distinguished between the death penalty for the murderer and the confinement to one of the cities of refuge for the manslayer. The LORD also deemed intentional homicide righteous in two circumstances. Perhaps you would agree we are already witnessing clues to answering the question of logic pertaining to the interpretation of Exodus 20:13.

This is at least the case in the Mosaic Law. Remember, the Mosaic Law is exclusively for the nation of Israel. We'll proceed now to find whether Christ has a similar view of intentional homicide in regards to the rest of the world. In other words, are there other situational contexts that are consistently found throughout the entire Biblical narrative in which intentional homicide is also deemed righteous rather than immoral or sinful? Before we embark on this search, we will first become familiar with the dispensational approach which will be the format we shall utilize during this inquiry.

7

DISPENSATIONAL APPROACH

W e 21st century Christians share a similar flaw with the folks of the 1st century church. I am speaking particularly of the original Jewish converts who were persuaded that Jesus of Nazareth was indeed the long awaited Messiah, the Anointed One of Israel. The term we use in English for His title of Messiah is "Christ," which is derived from the Greek translation of "anointed one." The failure to understand and embrace the total implication of this special designation, as foretold in the Hebrew Scriptures, is the basis for our common error.

After hearing Jesus Christ explain how He would suffer, be killed, then rise again, Peter basically chewed out the Lord by saying, "Far be it from You, Lord; this shall not happen to You!" Before Peter could figuratively remove his foot from his mouth, the Lord verbally spanked the disciple by replying, "Get behind Me, Satan! You are an offense to Me, for you are not mindful of the things of God, but the things of men" (Matthew 16:21-23).

Peter is well known for quickly speaking which commonly led to problems, but comprehending the root cause of this specific response to Jesus is crucial. Peter and the other disciples were expecting the Messiah to arrive as the Warrior King of Israel (John

1:41-49). This was a legitimate hope because the Hebrew Scriptures teach that concept of Him. They expected Him to fulfill the roles of the king originally requested by the nation in 1 Samuel 8:20: "That we also may be like all the nations, and that our king may judge us and go out before us and fight our battles."

The idea Messiah would arrive to serve, suffer, and sacrifice Himself for the sins of the world was utterly absurd to these Jewish believers. I can envision Peter and his friends articulating their feelings to this concept in the vernacular of our day: "That's just all kind of wrong!"

Yet, the truth is that the Older Testament also teaches the Anointed One would indeed fulfill that function. For instance, the prophet Isaiah explained how the One called the "Arm of the LORD" will suffer and die as a sacrifice to atone for the sin of man (Isaiah 52:13-53:12). Isaiah 51:9-10 clarifies the Arm of the LORD is God Himself. Evidently, the original disciples either did not remember those portions of Scripture or intentionally chose not to embrace them.

Likewise, we 21st century believers are guilty of clinging to one function of the Christ while ignoring the other. Typically, we are comfortable with His role as the Lamb of God, the meek and gentle Savior. We readily envision Jesus as the One who preached love and peace on earth. Like the disciples, we too squirm and balk at any idea of Jesus appearing to contradict those concepts. The discussion of Jesus' place as Israel's Warrior King and His view on the use of deadly force and killing is definitely one of controversy in this age.

As a result, we sometimes wrongly dichotomize God within the two testaments of the Bible. When the Older Testament Scriptures are used to demonstrate God's perspective on killing, the typical response is: "That's the God of the Old Testament." Another reply may be: "The God of the Old Testament is of wrath and the God of the New Testament is of grace."

The truth is the God of both testaments is the same God (Malachi 3:6). The text contained in the entire Bible was ultimately inspired by the Spirit of Christ. It's His perspective displayed through all of the sacred writings.

In order to answer this accusation of a dichotomized God, I will demonstrate the consistency of Christ's view on killing in both the Older and Newer testaments. My goal is to help the individual understand the God of both Testaments has not "repented" or changed His mind on this important subject. We'll also reap the additional benefit of determining the best translation and interpretation of Exodus 20:13. This will require an investigation of the Bible from the beginning of Scripture in Genesis to the last book, Revelation. In other words, this will demand a dispensational study of the entire 66 books of the Bible.

If you do not subscribe to the dispensational view of the Bible, particularly in regards to the relationship between Israel and the church, please don't stop here. My objective is to use the dispensations as a chronological structure or format as we examine the Scriptures. We will view various situations involving homicide and the time period, or dispensation, in which they occurred. As we study the sacred writings, I will note the dispensation in which that particular passage is located. The idea is to search the Scriptures from the beginning to the end in order to determine if the Bible is consistent in regards to God's perspective on killing.

Dr. Charles C. Ryrie gives us a good description of Dispensationalism in his book *Dispenationalism Today*. Dr. Ryrie states, "To summarize: Dispensationalism views the world as a household run by God. In this household-world God is dispensing or administering its affairs according to His will and in various stages or revelation in the **process of time**."(emphasis mine) "These various stages mark off the distinguishably different economies in the outworking of His total purpose, and these economies are the dispensations."(29)

The consensus of most theologians that hold the dispensationalist view of Scripture is that there are seven dispensations:

#1 The Dispensation of Innocence or Freedom (Genesis 1:28-3:6)

#2 The Dispensation of Conscience or Self-Determination (Genesis 4:1-8:14)

#3 The Dispensation of Civil Government (Genesis 8:15-11:9)

#4 The Dispensation of Promise or Patriarchal Rule (Genesis 11:10-Exodus 18:27)

#5 The Dispensation of the Mosaic Law (Exodus 19:1-Acts 1:26)

#6 The Dispensation of Grace (Acts 2:1- Revelation 19:21); and

#7 The Dispensation of the Millennium occurs as soon as Christ returns in Revelation 19 and destroys the enemies of Jerusalem. Revelation 20 describes the 1000 year reign of Christ where He will rule the world from Jerusalem as King of Kings.(30)

Notice how the dispensations flow with the chronological order of history in which God has progressively revealed Himself to man via His word. It is paramount we use this structure to ascertain God's perspective on killing and to conclude whether it has changed throughout the ages or if it has remained consistent in the course of time. However, I am compelled to further explain the importance of the dispensational view in regards to Israel's relationship with the rest of the world.

Notice the fifth dispensation is called the Dispensation of the Mosaic Law. It's critical we understand that the Law given through the prophet Moses is exclusively for the nation of Israel. The LORD provided the Law for His redeemed national people. Although some of its precepts are mentioned and carried over into the Newer Testament, He doesn't hold any other nation or entity, including the church, accountable to the Mosaic Law.

Having clarity of its exclusivity will prove crucial particularly when we investigate the offenses requiring capital punishment and Israel's rules of war located in the Dispensation of the Mosaic Law. Finally, we'll begin our quest with a dispensational examination of the Scriptures focused specifically on what they teach on Christ's perspective of the death penalty.

8

THE DEATH PENALTY

K arla Faye Tucker went to trial in a Texas court in 1984 for a gruesome, double murder she committed in 1983. According to the law in Texas, this particular incident warranted a Capital Murder charge because it occurred while in the process of burglarizing a home and more than one person was murdered. The prosecuting District Attorney sought the maximum sentence, the death penalty. Tucker and her accomplices were convicted for the murders and all received the death penalty as their punishment.

While she awaited the results of her request for a retrial and appeals, Tucker was imprisoned in the Mountain View Unit in Gatesville, Texas. Once the appellate courts completely rejected the appeals in the late 1990's, her case became very popular. This was due to the fact she would be the first woman put to death in the United States since 1984 and in Texas since 1863. It also became public that Tucker claimed to have become a believer in Jesus Christ while she was in prison while awaiting her execution. The attention drawn to this case moved beyond the borders of the U.S., even to Pope John II and the Italian Prime Minister.

Tucker's execution date was set for February 3, 1998. Tucker and many others appealed with the State of Texas on Tucker's behalf to have her death sentence reduced to life in prison. Nonetheless, the request was denied on January 28, 1998. Tucker was moved on February 2, 1998, to the Texas execution prison facility in Huntsville, Texas. She was executed there by lethal injection on February 3, 1998.(31)

The debate on the morality of the death penalty was kindled during this period while Tucker anticipated her execution. I remember viewing on television the people who chose to show their opposition of this form of penal sentencing by carrying picket signs that read, "thou shall not kill." This obviously was an accusation that the government's administration of capital punishment violates the command in Exodus 20:13. However, does that argument have any standing based upon Biblical evidence? Our search for the best interpretation and intended meaning of that passage continues. We move forward with a dispensational exploration of the Scriptures to discover God's consistent perspective on the death penalty.

Dispensation of Innocence or Freedom

God/Adam

Our investigation begins with Genesis 2:15-17 which is revelation located in the Dispensation of Innocence or Freedom since sin and death had not yet entered the world. God had finished the process of His creation but Adam was still alone without a mate. Adam was placed in the garden of Eden to tend and keep it. According to Genesis 2:9, the LORD also made trees in the garden that were pleasant to look at and as a provision for food. The tree of life and the tree of the knowledge of good and evil were also located in the garden.

In verse 16 God told Adam he was free to eat from any of the trees. However, He gave a command in verse 17 forbidding Adam from eating the fruit grown from the tree of knowledge of good and evil. In Genesis 2:17b, the LORD assigned the following penalty for the violation of this command:

17b) for in the day that you eat of it you shall surely die."

We see early in history, within the first two dispensational periods that God established His justice when He commanded it was forbidden to partake of the tree of knowledge of good and evil. He took the violation of His justice so serious that He allocated a death penalty as the punishment. In other words, rebellion would require that man pay the ultimate cost.

Genesis 2 ends with God fabricating Eve from Adam's ribs to be his mate. Most of us are familiar with the narrative in Genesis 3 which covers the event when Adam and Eve eventually violate God's command by eating from the forbidden tree. The Lord refused to waver and compromise His justice so the death penalty was administered.

Although the couple did not immediately encounter physical death, there was a death that occurred that day. They experienced spiritual and relational death, that is, relational separation from God the moment they broke the commandment. The process of physical death also started because sin and death had entered the world (Romans 5:12). This point is also the beginning of the Dispensation of Conscience or Self-Determination for they had gained the knowledge of good and evil.

The sin of Adam and the resulting death penalty did not involve Adam and Eve alone. The sentence of death was passed on to every one of their descendants. Because of their breach of God's command, all of us come into the world not only flawed, but spiritually dead and relationally separated from God. We also experience physical death as a result. The theological term for this process is "Imputed Sin."

However, remember I wrote about the grace of God in the Older Testament. God demonstrated His mercy by forcing Adam and Eve to leave the garden. This was to remove them from the temptation to eat from the tree of life and live forever in their fallen state (Genesis 3:22-24). We'll discuss their eviction in more detail during our study of the Scriptures in regards to self-defense in Chapter Nine.

On the other hand, Genesis 3:14-15 reveals His grace by disclosing His plan for salvation immediately after the fall. The Seed of the woman will come and make things right again by fatally wounding the serpent and saving man. We will discuss He who shall eventually come and execute God's rescue plan later in this book.

It didn't take long to see some of the consequences of Adam's sin. Adam and Eve had two sons, Cain and Abel. Genesis 4 contains the record of the first murder case in human history. In a fit of apparent jealousy Cain killed his brother (Genesis 4:8). We can only attempt to imagine the pain the first couple experienced when their son was murdered by his own brother. In addition, they had to wrestle with the fact that this horrible act and the death sentence that followed was a direct consequence of their sin in the Garden of Eden.

Dispensation of Civil Government

Noah

In Genesis Chapter 9 we find the beginning God's Dispensation of Civil Government to mankind, that is, the right and responsibility to rule and direct the affairs of people. This same chapter also contains the record of Noah and his family after they survived the flood. He and his sons had pleased God with their obedience to Him. They had taken God at His word on the impending flood, built the ark, and saved their families and the animals. In Genesis 9:1 God told Noah and his sons to "be fruitful and multiply, and fill the earth." He also revealed to them that all things on the earth are subject to their authority.

A common error we humans commit is to think the Creator of all things is somewhat naïve, unaware of the brutal aspects of mankind. Even we who believe in His Son as Savior are not necessarily exempt from such faulty thinking. Yet, as in all things, God has a much more practical perspective about the reality of life than most people understand. Because the LORD is all knowing, He was keenly aware of life's potential struggles and the brutality to be experienced in it. God knew humanity would require to be governed by man. Man would need justice to be served temporally, or in the present, and not only eternally, with the punishment of hell.

Having placed government over people in the hands of people, the LORD proceeded to establish His guiding principles for such authority. In regards to human government, it is interesting God began by decreeing the penalty for the one who illicitly kills another man. Genesis 9:5-6a-c reveals the following:

> 5) "Surely for your lifeblood I will demand a reckoning; from the hand of every beast I will require it, and from the hand of man. From the hand of every man's brother I will require the life of man.
>
> 6a-c) "Whoever sheds man's blood, By man his blood shall be shed; for in the image of God He made man."

God established His justice in Genesis 2. When Adam and Eve violated His law, "God" administered the death penalty. In Genesis 9:5-6a-c, God designed a temporal judicial principle which states the act of murdering another person is a violation of the justice within the context of human government. As a result, God removed Himself as the One to administer the death penalty. Notice in verse 6b to whom God assigned the duty of dealing out the punishment:

> 6a-b) "Whoever sheds man's blood, By man his blood shall be shed."

God delegated to man the authority to act as the executioner of the death penalty. Man has been given the mandate to govern the actions of men. More specifically, man has the legal right to end the life of the one who murders another man.

In the United States legal system, we have several levels of appellate courts. The U.S. Supreme Court has the ultimate authority to examine any appealed case and decide if the actions taken, including punishment, are justified or contrary to the first and highest law of the land, the U.S. Constitution. Genesis 9:5-6a-b reveals the rendering of a judgment from the highest court in the universe. The Judge of the Heavenly Court has decreed this principle in regards to punishing the murderer.

Notice I used the word "murder" to describe the violation addressed in Genesis 9:6 although the translation is actually the English word "shed." My interpretation is based on contextual investigation, which as we learned earlier is crucial to find the author's intended use or meaning of any word or phrase. We have an excellent opportunity in this passage to demonstrate an application of the law of non-contradiction. Allow me to explain.

The phrase "shed man's blood" is used throughout verse 6. I think we would agree "shed man's blood" has a broad definition of "taking the life of another human being." Unfortunately, the vague meaning can cause a similar problem in interpretation as we have in Exodus 20:13. One may understand God is condemning all intentional homicide. However, the LORD commanded in verse 6b for man to intentionally take the life of the killer described earlier in the verse. We have a contradiction to the general interpretation which means it's illogical.

When we study the use of the phrase in the full context of verse 6, it appears the shedding of man's blood has two different intended meanings in this one verse. The first use of this phrase in verse 6a seems to convey an unjustified or illegal killing. We are able to assume this meaning by observing 6b. The second use of the same phrase in verse 6b is applied in the command by God to shed the blood of the offender in 6a. Since God's commands are good and just, we can conclude the shedding of man's blood in 6a is "evil," while the shedding of the blood of the offender in 6b is righteous. Therefore, there are two different intended meanings of the words "shed man's blood" in Genesis 9:6.

As I mentioned earlier, we could substitute the English verb "kill" for "sheds man's blood" in verse 6 and still be able to interpret the dual meanings. The word "kill" has a similar broad definition of causing the death of another. Yet, the vague connotation of the word can lead to potentially significant problems in interpretation. We can still reach a more accurate intended meaning of the word "kill," if it were utilized in Genesis 9:6, after a thorough contextual investigation.

It's also important to keep verse 6b in context with verse 6c because we find God's heart motive for the establishment of the death penalty:

6c) "For in the image of God he made man."

The word "for" indicates God is making a connection with the immediate previous command. He's explaining why such a harsh punishment is warranted for illegally shedding another man's blood. Man is made in the image of God. We are taught this truth in earlier verses like Genesis 1:26 and Genesis 5:1 as well.

Man is different from the rest of creation. We are not like God in the sense of nature for He is divine. We are made in His image in the sense of mind, will, and emotion. You and I are special to God. For instance, each verse in Genesis 1:10, 12, 18, 21, and 25 ends with "And God saw that it was good." This was His reaction to His creation during the first five days. However, on the sixth day God created man. Genesis 1:31 reveals His response after creating man:

31) Then God saw everything that He had made, and indeed it was **very** good. (emphasis mine)

God is teaching us that human life is special to Him. It's so precious in His sight He is willing to take the life of the person who murders the one made in His image. My mentor, Tom Rodgers, expounded on this concept to me by saying: "Charlie, we should cherish life, but we cannot worship it." If we allow the murderer to escape the ultimate consequence we actually de-value human life. We turn our worship away from the Giver of Life to the life He created.

There's another significant piece of truth in this context. As we continue to read on to verse 7, we witness a relative purpose for man in regards to man's relationship with the earth. God gave the following command to Noah and his family in Genesis 9:7:

7) And as for you, be fruitful and multiply; Bring forth abundantly in the earth And multiply in it."

God's plan for man is to subdue the earth and have dominion over it. I believe murder is also in direct violation of God's order for man to be fruitful and multiply. Illegally taking a human life could be viewed as an attempt to thwart this objective. This is another powerful reason why the death penalty is the warranted punishment for those who commit such an offense.

Another interesting observation is the place in history where we find God commanding this death penalty in Genesis 9. This is prior to the establishment of the nation of Israel and His provision of the Mosaic Law to His national people. We should then interpret the command as a universal principle for all governments of the world, regardless of time era, concerning the punishment for the murderer. For, as we previously emphasized, the Mosaic Law was exclusive guidance to the nation of Israel and we have already witnessed that the fate for the murderer in Numbers and Deuteronomy is death.

There is much of the Law still to be examined. As we have already seen in Numbers and Deuteronomy, the LORD demonstrated deep care and concern for His national people through demanding the death penalty for the murderer and a strict penalty for even the man-slayer who unintentionally killed another Israelite. Let's survey the rest of the Mosaic Law to find if God restricted capital punishment for the murderer. Were the children of Israel who were convicted of other offenses also in danger of losing their lives?

Dispensation of the Mosaic Law

Moses

Several centuries prior to Moses' entrance into history, God selected Abraham to be the father of His chosen national people, Israel. The population of the nation reached 70 during the life time of Joseph, Abraham's great-grandson. There was a great famine in the land and Israel suffered along with the other nations. Joseph and Israel were eventually led by God into Egypt to deliver them from starvation and as a form of isolation and protection from the surrounding pagan worship in Canaan.

Although Israel experienced good times while under the leadership of Joseph and the Egyptian Pharaoh, the tide later turned for the nation and they were ultimately enslaved in the land. Moses was raised up by God to be their deliverer who later led his people out of slavery through the LORD's power. The Hebrew people were in Egypt for about 400 years where the nation grew to a population of over two million. As we discussed earlier, Israel was judged for their failure to take the land of promise due to their fear of its inhabitants. The nation ended up in the wilderness and in need of organization and civil leadership.

God began to give the Law to Israel through the prophet Moses. The initial portion of the Mosaic Law is recorded in Exodus 20 which includes the Decalogue, or the Ten Commandments. The other writings of Moses included in the Dispensation of the Mosaic Law are Leviticus, Numbers, and Deuteronomy. In Exodus 21 God began to provide guidance in regards to punishment for certain offenses. More specifically, He gave the Law which identified the criminal and religious offenses that warranted the death penalty. According to the Mosaic Law, the offender was to be put to death for the following violations:

1. Murder–Exodus 21:12,14; Leviticus 24:17,21b
2. Kidnapping–Exodus 21:16
3. Striking one's father or mother–Exodus 21:15
4. Cursing one's father or mother–Exodus 21:17; Leviticus 20:9
5. Causing the death of an unborn child via violence– Exodus 21:22-25
6. Failure to confine a known dangerous ox and it kills another person–Exodus 21:28-29
7. The son who is rebellious, glutton, and drunkard– Deuteronomy 21:18-21
8. Sorcery–Exodus 22:18
9. Man or a woman who is a medium or has familiar spirits– Leviticus 20:27
10. Bestiality–Exodus 22:19; Leviticus 20:15-16
11. Sacrificing to or serving any god other than The LORD– Exodus 22:20; Leviticus 17:2-5
12. Afflicting any widow or fatherless child–Exodus 22:22-24
13. Sacrificing children to Molech–Leviticus 20:2
14. Adultery–Leviticus 20:10; Deuteronomy 22:22-24
15. Incest–Leviticus 20:11-12,14
16. Homosexuality–Leviticus 20:13
17. Sexual Assault of a betrothed woman– Deuteronomy 22:25-26
18. A woman playing the harlot while still in her father's house–Deuteronomy 22:23-24

19. Daughter of a priest who prostitutes herself–Leviticus 21:9

20. Failure to submit to declared legal punishment–
    Deuteronomy 17:8-12

21. Blasphemy–Leviticus 24:11-16,23

22. Violating the Sabbath–Exodus 31:14-15; Numbers 15:32-36

23. Non-priests who approach the tabernacle while it is being
    moved–Numbers 1:51

24. Enticing others to serve other gods–Deuteronomy
    13:6-10,12-18

25. An enticing prophet and dreamer of dreams–
    Deuteronomy 13:1-5

26. Falsely prophesying in the LORD's name–
    Deuteronomy 18:20-22

There are other violations spoken of in the Law that possibly carried the death sentence. These offenses are assigned the punishment of "shall be cut off from among his people." Some theologians, such as Dr. Charles C. Ryrie, hold the view that this means to be cut off by banishment or execution.(32)

Exodus 31:14-15 calls for the death penalty when the Sabbath is violated. However, it also explains the violator shall be cut off from among his people. In Leviticus 20:1-6, God gave such a command for those of Israel or strangers who "give their descendants to Molech." According to verse 2, they are to be put to death by stoning. The LORD provided the consequence for this violation found in verse 3:

> 3) 'I will set My face against that man, and will cut him off from his people, because he has given some of his descendants to Molech, to defile My sanctuary and profane My holy name."

71

According to Leviticus 20:4-6, the LORD assigned the same penalty of being "cut off from his people" for those who turn a blind eye to such a heinous offense and for those who turn to mediums and familiar spirits.

Additional offenses that warranted the penalty of being cut off from his people are:

1. Male who is not circumcised–Genesis 17:14
2. Eating leavened bread during the Feast of Unleavened Bread–Exodus 12:15
3. Misuse of anointing oil–Exodus 30:31-33
4. Engaging in ritual animal sacrifices outside of the temple–Leviticus 17:1-9
5. Consuming blood–Leviticus 17:10-14
6. Sexual intercourse with a menstruating woman–Leviticus 20:18
7. Eating the sacrifice of peace offerings while being ritually unclean–Leviticus 7:20
8. Waiting too long to eat the sacrifices of peace offerings–Leviticus 19:5-8
9. Attending the temple while in an unclean state–Numbers 19:13

Although God is not hesitant to assign the death penalty to various violations, He is critical about the justification of its use. The LORD gave the command in Exodus 23:7 that no innocent or righteous persons should be put to death. This particular principle will be re-visited when we study the Newer Testament in regards to the sentencing of Jesus Christ to be crucified. In Deuteronomy 17:4, God demanded the execution of a diligent investigation so that the indictment is certain and true before assigning the death penalty.

It's also forbidden to execute any person based solely upon the testimony of one witness (Numbers 35:30). The testimony of two or three witnesses is required for the conviction of any offense that would call for the death penalty (Deuteronomy 17:6,19:15). According to the Scriptures, direct witness testimony is not only material in a death penalty case, it is mandatory. As a form of accountability the "hands of the witnesses" shall be first against the person who is condemned to death, according to Deuteronomy 17:7. In addition, it would be a trip to the executioner for the person who commits perjury and gives false testimony that would send an innocent person to their death (Deuteronomy 19:15-21).

God had chosen Israel as His people and delivered them from slavery in Egypt. As part of His covenant with Israel, He gave them the Mosaic Law as a code of conduct to follow in order to please Him. The LORD elected them to be His folk, and to be set apart from the other nations (Leviticus 21:4). Through obedience to His Law, Israel would demonstrate holiness which would showcase the LORD's character and His unique relationship with Israel.

God was very strict in regards to their obedience which is evident by His expansion of the death penalty for other offenses in addition to murder. However, the LORD revealed in Numbers 35:31-34 another significant concern pertaining to the victim's blood of any illegal killing:

> 31) 'Moreover you shall take no ransom for the life of a murderer who is guilty of death, but he shall surely be put to death. 32) 'And you shall take no ransom for him who has fled to his city of refuge, that he may return to dwell in the land before the death of the priest. 33) 'So you shall not pollute the land where you are; for blood defiles the land, and no atonement can be made for the land, for the blood that is shed on it, except by the blood of him who

shed it. 34) 'Therefore do not defile the land which you inhabit, in the midst of which I dwell; for I the LORD dwell among the children of Israel.'"

Evidently the blood of the innocent defiled the land in Israel. For this reason no ransom shall be taken to let the murderer live or for the manslayer to return to his land of possession before the death of the high priest. The only atonement that can be made on behalf of the land would be by the shed blood of the murderer. According to verse 34, this was particularly important to the LORD for He actually dwelt in the land with the children of Israel.

God's reputation as a loving Father to His children was also at stake. His provision to Israel with the 613 commandments and the harsh consequences for violating them was for reasons similar to why we impart rules and punishment for our own children. By following the rules they would protect themselves from self-destruction and live in prosperity (Deuteronomy 29:9). Likewise, we discipline our children for their disobedience in hope that it will deter them from ruining their lives by committing future violations. Figuratively speaking, we want to steer them from the "landmines" that await them in the field of life that can destroy them and prevent them from experiencing a thriving life.

The LORD had another important objective for such severe punishment as death. He desired for Israel to "hear and fear." Deuteronomy 13:11 follows the command to kill the one who enticed others to follow other gods. Verse 11 reads:

11) "So all Israel shall hear and fear, and not again do such wickedness as this among you."

Deuteronomy 17:13 follows the command in verse 12 to put to death the one who ignores their assigned judgment. Verse 13 reads:

74

13) "And all the people shall hear and fear, and no longer act presumptuously."

Deuteronomy 19:20 follows the command located in verses 16-19 to execute the one who commits perjury against his brother. Verse 20 reads:

20) "And those who remain shall hear and fear, and hereafter they shall not commit such evil among you."

An additional purpose of the death penalty was to induce fear in the hearts of God's people in order to preclude future offenses against Him. The individual's contemplation on potentially losing his life through capital punishment would ultimately aid in fulfilling the LORD's goals for His nation. As we move forward with our study, we shall observe that God's objective to "hear and fear" is actually a consistent principle taught in the Scriptures, particularly in some of the inspired writings of the Apostle Paul. But we'll first move to the times of the kings to investigate their role and authority in administering the death penalty.

David and Solomon

In order to totally grasp the role and authority of the kings, it is crucial we first examine 1 Samuel 8:1-22. Prior to the time of Israel's first king, the prophet Samuel appointed three of his sons as judges over Israel. Unfortunately, all three were found to be corrupt as they took bribes and perverted justice. The elders of Israel then approached Samuel and said to him in verse 5:

> 5) "Look, you are old, and your sons do not walk in your ways. Now make us a king to judge us like all the nations."

The leaders of Israel envied the surrounding monarchies or king-led nations. They were ready to give the king full authority to judge them. The kings of the nations sometimes heard cases and rendered decisions as a one-man jury panel. He then determined innocence or guilt and passed judgment which included capital punishment. Israel desired to experience the same type of judicial system and this greatly displeased the prophet. However, the LORD clarified the deeper issue to Samuel in verse 7:

> 7) And the LORD said to Samuel, "Heed the voice of the people in all that they say to you; for they have not rejected you, but they have rejected Me, that I should not reign over them."

The LORD God of Israel always wanted to be the "King" of Israel. He reminded Samuel of the nation's disobedience that had occurred ever since their deliverance from Egypt. They had forsaken the LORD and served other Gods. In fact, their request for a king to judge them had much more meaning than an insult to the prophet. It was ultimately the nation's refusal to submit to the LORD as their king.

The LORD directed Samuel to warn the people through explaining the future negative actions of their ruling king. Samuel's admonishment is found in verses 11-18 which ends with the prediction that the people would eventually cry out to the LORD because of the king they had chosen. Even after hearing the detailed behavior they could expect from a monarch, the people still replied in verses 19-20:

> 19) Nevertheless the people refused to obey the voice of Samuel; and they said, "No, but we will have a king over us, 20)"that we also may be like all the nations, and that our king may judge us and go out before us and fight our battles."

Notice the additional function the people expected their king to perform. He was to lead them into the field and fight their battles for them. Isn't it interesting the LORD had fulfilled both of these roles for Israel since He rescued them from Egypt? How quickly we humans forget. Understanding these two expected functions of the king is significant particularly in regards to Jesus Christ and His future relationship to Israel.

Due to its connection to the king's authority to assign punishment for evil or rebellious acts, we will, for now, draw our attention exclusively to the king's role as judge over his people. More specifically, we will examine how King David and King Solomon fleshed out their responsibility as judge of Israel in three separate situations recorded in 1 Kings 1-2.

King David's life and his rule over Israel were coming to an end and the throne would soon need a successor. The LORD previously gave instruction to David and the prophet Nathan that David's son, Solomon, would be the one to receive the throne. David's other son, Adonijah, had different plans.

According to 1 Kings 1:11, Adonijah took the initiative and declared himself king of Israel without the approval of David. He sacrificed animals and publicly called himself David's successor. He was smart enough not to invite those who were loyal to David to any of the festivities. Word of Adonijah's treason eventually reached the ears of the prophet Nathan who knew Solomon was the one chosen by God to take the throne. This takeover attempt also eventually caught the attention of King David and Solomon.

The second situation that concerned King David is presented in 1 Kings 2:5. David gave instruction to Solomon to remember another man named Joab who had done evil to two of the king's army commanders, Abner the son of Ner, and Amasa the son of Jether. Joab murdered both of these men by alluring them close to himself then stabbing them in the stomach, fatally wounding them (2 Samuel 3: 23-27, 2 Samuel 20: 7-10). We shall soon witness how Joab would suffer the consequences for his acts of murder.

There is one more person who would face the justice of Solomon as well. This third case involved a man named Shimei. According to 2 Samuel 16:4-13, Shimei, of the house of Saul, took the opportunity to verbally bash and insult King David in the past. He even picked up stones and threw them at the king while David was moving along with his servants and his mighty men. Shimei called David a "bloodthirsty man" and a "rogue." He also made claims that the LORD had delivered the kingdom to Absalom, David's other son. We will revisit this situation with Shimei in Chapter 10 when we study David as the warrior king. However, now that we are familiar with these three predicaments, let us return our attention to Adonijah.

Adonijah ultimately learned Solomon had been formally anointed King of Israel (1 Kings 1:50-52). As a result, he became afraid of what might happen next so he sought a seemingly safe place. He went in and took hold of the horns of the altar. Adonijah then sent the following words to Solomon found in verse 51:

51) "Let King Solomon swear to me that he will not put his servant to death with the sword."

Notice that Adonijah acknowledged the king's authority to legitimately sentence him to death for his act of treason. Solomon decided to show mercy and give Adonijah the chance to prove himself as a "worthy man." But if wickedness was found in him, he would die. 1 Kings 2:10-25 reveals it didn't take long for Adonijah to show his true motive.

King David died and Solomon received the kingdom. Adonijah viewed David's death as an opportunity to make his way to the throne in a more covert manner. He went to Bethsheba, Solomon's mother, and asked for the hand of Abishag the Shunammite as his wife. Bethsheba exposed the request to Solomon who recognized it as a plot to become an heir by marriage with the intent to take the throne. Even worse for Adonijah, Solomon evidently viewed his plan as an act of wickedness.

King Solomon sentenced Adonijah to death. Solomon demonstrated confidence in the righteousness of his order by leaving his own life to God if it were not legitimate. King Solomon executed his justice by sending out Benaiah, son of Jehoiada, who struck down Adonijah and he died. The Prophet/King Solomon lived on afterward so we can conclude that his decree of capital punishment was indeed considered to be justified by the LORD.

As a sidebar observation, view with me 1 Kings 2:26-27. Solomon addressed Abiathar the priest who had been in league with Adonijah and Joab during the attempted coup of Solomon's throne. He plainly told Abiathar the punishment he justly deserved in verse 26:

> 26) "you are deserving of death; but I will not put you to death at this time, because you carried the ark of the Lord GOD before my father David, and because you were afflicted every time my father was afflicted."

According to verse 27, instead of death, Solomon removed Abiathar from being priest to the Lord. Regardless of the mercy he showed, Solomon again communicated he had the authority to administer the death penalty.

1 Kings 2:28-34 exposes Solomon's response to the murderer, Joab. Joab heard about the demise of Adonijah and surely remembered he had not only murdered two of David's commanders but he also defected to Adonijah during his attempt to take the throne. It is understandable why he would be concerned for his own life. In a desperate attempt to save his life, Joab also went to the tabernacle of the LORD and took hold of the horns of the altar. King Solomon sent Benaiah to strike him down.

Joab would not come out to face the executioner so King Solomon commanded Benaiah to go into the tabernacle and strike him down and bury him. The loyal Benaiah obeyed the king's command and killed Joab. Solomon provided clarity on why justice was served by putting Joab to death in 1 Kings 2:31-33:

> 31) Then the king said to him, "Do as he has said, and strike him down and bury him, that you may take away from me and from the house of my father the innocent blood which Joab shed. 32) "So the LORD will return his blood on his head, because he struck down two men more righteous and better then he, and killed them with the sword-Abner the son of Ner, the commander of the army of Israel, and Amasa the son of Jether, the commander of the army of Judah-though my father David did not know it. 33) "Their blood shall therefore return upon the head of Joab and upon the head of his descendants forever. But upon David and his descendants, upon his house and his throne, there shall be peace forever from the LORD."

Joab had committed murder while under the authority of King David. Although David was not privy to his intentions, this evidently brought the blood of the murdered men upon Solomon and the house of David. The innocent blood of those murdered would be placed upon the head of Joab and his descendents forever after justice was served through his execution. On the other hand, there would be peace from the LORD upon David and his descendents, upon his house and his throne forever. It is interesting that Solomon brought the LORD's peace upon his house and his throne through the administration of the death penalty.

Let us now observe how King Solomon dealt with Shimei in 1 Kings 2:36-46. The king called for Shimei and made a new commandment for him. He once again showed mercy to this rebel rouser by deferring the death penalty as long as Shimei remained obedient to one specific command. He was ordered to build himself a house in Jerusalem and stay there. If he violated the command by even crossing the Brook Kidron he would be put to death and his blood would be on his own head. Shimei agreed to the arrangement and even swore an oath to the LORD to abide by the law.

Shimei lived in Jerusalem for three years without a violation until two of his slaves ran away to Gath. After receiving information of the location of the slaves, he traveled to Gath where he collected them and returned to Jerusalem. King Solomon was briefed about Shimei's trip and immediately addressed him for violating the command.

Solomon started by reminding Shimei that he had sworn by the LORD to keep the commandment and that Shimei also had commented on the order by declaring, "The word I have heard is good." The king added that Shimei broke an oath of the LORD and the commandment Solomon had given him. In other words, King Solomon considered Shimei's violation of the command as an act of disobedience to the LORD. The wickedness that Shimei had done to King David returned on his own head.

Notice what Solomon surmised about the future of his kingdom as a result of carrying out the just punishment of death on Shimei in 1 Kings 2:45:

> 45) "But King Solomon shall be blessed, and the throne of David shall be established before the LORD forever."

King Solomon again called on loyal Benaiah who went and executed Shimei. Verse 46 ends with these words:

> 46) "Thus the kingdom was **established** (emphasis mine) in the hand of Solomon."

Solomon was to be blessed in contrast to Shemei's curse. In addition, we have observed in two situations where there's indeed a significant connection between the king's justice and the establishment of his kingdom. We shall gain even more clarity on this principle as we observe some of King Solomon's wisdom writings.

Solomon

We shall first examine some of Solomon's wisdom writings contained in the book of Proverbs. King Solomon was one of three authors of this book which also falls in the Dispensation of the Mosaic Law. The purpose of the Proverbs was to provide guidance and wisdom with the goal of honing the skills needed for living well. For instance, Proverbs 29:4 reveals very clear instruction for the king or ruler of any land who wants to have success and stability during their reign:

4) The king establishes the land by justice, But he who receives bribes overthrows it.

This specific Proverb describes a relationship between the justice of the king and the status of the land. When the king ensures that justice is being served, the land is established. The New American Standard Version Bible has translated the word as "stability," rather than "established," as that which is brought to the land when justice exists.(33) The law alone doesn't have the ability to produce order without enforcement by the government. Violations of the law must be prosecuted and the penalties must be administered in order for justice to be served. Only then will the land or kingdom be established and the citizens shall enjoy stability and order.

King Solomon finished the above verse with an interesting statement. The word "but" indicates the words following it would convey an idea in contrast to what he had just revealed. In other words, the land suffers when a king or the prosecuting authority receives a bribe. The purpose of the payment would be to persuade those in charge to compromise justice. An example response to the bribe would be the dismissal of a criminal case or reduction of the penal sentence absent of legal grounds. It's not difficult to detect corruption when blatant violations of the law are not pursued by the authorities. These scandalous acts are at times highly profiled to the public which may actually expedite the disestablishment of the land.

Of course King Solomon also knew the commands in Exodus 23:8 and Deuteronomy 16:19 forbidding the receiving of a bride for it perverts justice. As we reviewed earlier in this chapter, there is also a specific precept forbidding the acceptance of a ransom when a murder case is involved. Numbers 35:30 commands that the murderer shall be put to death but only on the testimony of two or more witnesses. Verse 31 also gives instruction on taking a ransom, money, or something of monetary value once the murderer is found guilty:

> 31) 'Moreover you shall take no ransom for the life of the murderer who is guilty of death, but he shall surely be put to death.

Numbers 35:32 also prohibits a person in authority from taking a ransom to allow the one convicted in a manslaughter case to return from a "city of refuge" prior to the death of the high priest. People are willing to pay to have their life or the life of another spared from the death penalty. This can be an enormous temptation for any judicial figure to exchange the righteous administration of justice for personal monetary gain.

As you can imagine, this corruption of law and order will eventually cause the stability and establishment of the land to deteriorate. The king will eventually, in one way or another, lose control of his kingdom and his right to rule. King Solomon taught more on the king's authority in Proverbs 20:2:

> 2) The wrath of the king is like the roaring lion; Whoever provokes him to anger sins against his own life.

What a great word picture King Solomon created here. The king's wrath or punishment is compared to a roaring lion. What image forms when you view a roaring lion in your mind's eye? I don't envision the scene of one petting him on the head and playing yarn games with him. I think it would be accurate to conclude that wasn't Solomon's intended meaning either.

The lion is already dangerous and deadly. If he is roaring, then he is not lounging around watching the lioness hunt for his food. He is demonstrating his powerful voice, his lethal fangs, and that it is his role to inflict punishment. Imagine the huge paws he possesses and how with a single swipe of his claws this roaring lion can cause death. He is ready for battle and ready to kill. But why is the lion roaring? Verse 2b provides the answer to this question.

I have seen lions in the zoo many times. They are typically peaceful and serene. On the other hand, there are frequently visitors of the zoo who want some excitement. The "thrill seeker" begins to taunt the lion and eventually reaches their intended result. The lion is provoked to the point he becomes angry. He becomes aggressive and rings out his booming voice. He roars as a response to their foolish provocation.

Proverbs 20:2b teaches that a king can also be provoked. What might provoke a king to the point that he would "lash out" in his wrath? I would venture to say the willful violation of his law would produce such a reaction. Rebellion is a figurative slap to the king's face but a literal attack on his sovereignty. The violator of the law is conveying to the authority that the king will not rule over him. The criminal says through his lawlessness:

"I will make my own rules and live by them and how dare you tell me how to live in your kingdom!"

King Solomon had something to say about this person who has chosen to provoke the king: That fool "sins against his own life." We'll later visit Scripture that reveals the connection between rebellion to the king and sin. However, notice also the provoker's life is somehow in danger.

Let's combine the two ideas in this verse. We have a roaring lion and the idea of the provoker's life being at stake. The possible consequence of rebellion could be physical death and the king is justified when he chooses to administer that punishment. Considering the above, it makes perfect sense that the word for "wrath" can also be translated "fear" or "terror" which is produced by the king's severe reprimand. It's far better to be in the king's favor because it is "like dew on the grass." It is refreshing and sustains the life of the citizen according to Proverbs 19:12.

Proverbs 16:14-15 also conveys the seriousness of being cross with the king as well as the blessing of being in his favor:

> 14) As messengers of death is the king's wrath, But a wise man will appease it.15) In the light of the king's face is life, And his favor is like a cloud of the latter rain.

Notice the comparisons Solomon made. When the individual brings himself under the king's wrath, death is the experience. On the other hand, the individual experiences life as that from a wonderful rain when he is in the king's favor. The king has so much authority and opportunity to bring a good experience to the individual's life. Regardless, goodness will come to the land even if the king's wrath is provoked and the individual's life is forfeited. This may prompt the following question: How does the ultimate penalty of death bring good to the people of the kingdom? Proverbs 20:8 and Proverbs 20:26 provide some clarification with the following:

> 8) A king who sits on the throne of judgment scatters all evil with his eyes.

> 26) A wise king sifts out the wicked, And brings the threshing wheel over them.

The wise king and his wrath provide for his people by ridding the land of evil and wickedness. There must be harsh penalties administered in order to produce fear in the hearts of those who have future intentions of rebellion such as breaking the laws of the land. The threshing wheel is a highly destructive mechanism. It crushes and takes the life away from that which it is attacking.

The idea conveyed is the king and his laws are for good to his land and his people. He brings security and stability out of chaos through the reality of his justice and wrath, which at times lashes out with lethal consequences. King Solomon continued to expose wisdom on this subject in Ecclesiastes 8:4-6:

> 4) Where the word of a king is, there is power; And who may say to him, "What are you doing?" 5) He who keeps his command will experience nothing harmful; And a wise man's heart discerns both time and judgment, 6) Because for every matter there is a time and judgment, Though the misery of man increases greatly.

Again we see there is power in the king's commands. Solomon reassured the obedient citizen that they have nothing to fear from the king for his wrath will not do them harm. I think we all would agree death is harmful. In Ecclesiastes 8:11 Solomon made another excellent point in regards to the prosecution of those who break the law:

> 11) Because the sentence against an evil work is not executed speedily, therefore the heart of the sons of men is fully set in them to do evil.

According to wise Solomon, when the king or government delays the execution of sentences for convicted criminals, the desired result is not captured. The ability to establish fear and deter future evil works is significantly hindered. Those who plan to commit crimes perceive the delay as one of weakness of the king or government and the procrastination actually encourages the furtherance of criminal activity. For this reason, every nation should seriously consider the principle of a speedy trial and swift execution of sentences.

King Solomon provided more mental-grid-developing guidance on killing in Ecclesiastes 3. We will visit that section of Scripture later when we investigate the use of deadly force in the contexts of war and policing. But for now we'll push on several years later to observe more examples of the death penalty being administered by godly men. Allow me first to set the historical context.

The kingdom of Israel experienced a split about 40 years after the beginning of Solomon's reign. The nation was divided into the northern kingdom of Israel and the southern kingdom of Judea. Both kingdoms were eventually ruled by several kings through the next few centuries. Not many of those kings were righteous. However, God also provided prophets or oracles during this period through whom He continued to give more revelation and prophecies for the future. One of the most distinguished prophets who served the LORD during this era was a man named Elijah.

Elijah

Join me now as we continue our study in 1 Kings 18. This section of the Bible still covers events located in the Dispensation of the Mosaic Law. Elijah the Tishbite, of the inhabitants of Gilead, was a prophet in the northern Kingdom of Israel around the year of 874 B.C.

A man named Ahab was king of Israel during the time of Elijah's ministry. Ahab was one of those unrighteous kings I mentioned earlier. He did more to provoke the LORD God of Israel to anger than all the kings before him for he led Israel into a dark place of worshipping false gods. We can view Elijah's plan to remedy this problem in 1 Kings 18:17-40.

In 1 Kings 18:17 King Ahab finally met up with Elijah and called him a "troubler of Israel." The prophet responded by revealing that Ahab and his father's house were the ones who actually troubled Israel. The indictment against Ahab and Israel was they forsook the commandments of the LORD and followed false gods known as the Baals. Because the children of Israel were deceived into idolatry, the prophet Elijah decided it was time for a "face-off."

Elijah called for all of Israel and the 450 prophets of Baal to meet him on Mount Carmel. He also summoned the 400 prophets of Asherah to be present. King Ahab agreed to the meeting and gathered all of them on the mount. Elijah pressed the people of Israel to make a decision: If the LORD is God, then follow Him or if Baal, then follow him. Elijah then commanded the prophets of Baal to prepare a bull for a burnt offering sacrifice. He prepared another bull for his own offering.

However, Elijah gave instructions to place the pieces of their selected animals on wood but they were not to place fire under it. If there is no fire how will a burnt offering be accomplished? That was exactly the question Elijah was attempting to rouse in the hearts of the spectators.

Elijah then set the standard for determining who was to be worshipped as the true God. Whichever god answered with fire for the sacrifice, He is God. He commanded the prophets to call on Baal to provide the fire for their offering. They called on Baal from the morning time until the evening. They yelled and jumped around the altar. Yet, they received no answer. They even cut themselves and caused bleeding just to get a reaction from Baal. Of course there never was an answer from the false god. This was no surprise to Elijah and now it was his turn.

Elijah did not immediately call upon the True and Living God to send the needed fire. He first had his sacrificial altar saturated with water. Elijah required for so much water to be poured on the altar that it was spilling over the edge. The altar was now ready for the demonstration. Elijah called upon the God of Abraham, Isaac, and Israel to show the people that He is God and Elijah was His servant. Fire came out of heaven and consumed the sacrifice, the altar, and all of the water. Nothing was left, including any doubt that the LORD is God.

After witnessing this glorious demonstration of His power, the people of Israel decided the LORD is God and they would serve Him alone. Elijah had accomplished his goal for the people. However, his business with the false prophets of Baal was not even close to being finished.

Had the prophets of Baal committed any crime heinous enough to forfeit their lives? Perhaps you can recollect one of the commandments in the Law that addresses the actions of the false prophets of Baal. Deuteronomy 13:6-10 and 12-18 command that those who entice the people to serve other gods shall be put to death. The 450 false prophets of Baal were clearly guilty of this offense. They allured the entire nation of Israel to turn from the True and Living God to worship and serve Baal.

Some people may have expected Elijah, a prophet and man of God, to certainly refuse to have all of those men executed. On the contrary, Elijah had Israel seize all of the 450 false prophets so that not even one of them escaped. 1 Kings 18:40 shares the action taken by the prophet:

40) So they seized them; and Elijah brought them down
to the Brook Kishon and executed them there.

Elijah administered the death penalty and took 450 lives. This
man of God faithfully carried out the just penalty that had been
assigned by God in the Law.

We must continue to investigate the rest of chapter 18 to interpret
God's perspective on the matter of Elijah's prosecution of the Law.
We should preface God's reaction to Elijah by first searching back
three years and six months prior to the execution of the false prophets
of Baal. According to1 Kings 17:1, Elijah said to King Ahab:

1) "As the LORD God of Israel lives, before whom I
stand, there shall not be dew or rain these years, except
at my word."

The drought was God's response to King Ahab's idolatrous
worship of Baal. The LORD had delegated to Elijah the authority to
determine when Israel would receive dew or rain again.

According to 1 Kings 18:41-45, immediately after Elijah executed the false prophets of Baal, Elijah warned Ahab to "go up, eat
and drink for there is the sound of abundance of rain." Elijah then
went to the top of Carmel and bowed down with his face between
his knees. The prophet told his servant to look toward the sea. A
small cloud was seen coming out of the sea which brought a large
amount of precipitation to the land. The Scripture describes it as
"a heavy rain." What was Elijah doing while he was bowed down?
The immediate text does not explicitly tell us but we can find the
explanation in James 5.

The contextual theme of the book of James is the obedient
response to God while experiencing trials and tribulations in our

lives. The epistle predominately addresses the life experience of the believer in Christ. Since prayer is an extremely significant discipline for the believer, James took time to provide guidance in that area. In regards to the Christian's prayer life James 5:16 states:

> 16) The effective, fervent prayer of a righteous man avails much.

Notice the prayer that will accomplish much comes from a "righteous" man. Again, this righteousness is declared upon the believer who endures faithfully through the trials of life (James 1:19-20). The apostle utilized Elijah's experience to further illustrate the relationship between the obedient status of the requester and the ultimate benefit of the prayer in James 5:17-18:

> 17) Elijah was a man with a nature like ours, and he prayed earnestly that it would not rain; and it did not rain on the land for three years and six months.18) And he prayed again, and the heaven gave rain, and the earth produced its fruit.

God listened to Elijah as he prayed to maintain the drought for three years and six months. He then prayed again which resulted in heaven giving rain and the earth produced its fruit. Therefore, we have ascertained the prophet was praying when he bowed down on top of Mount Carmel.

James' point is that Elijah was considered by God to be a righteous man. The LORD heard Elijah's prayer request and dispatched the rain as a response. This observation is extremely significant to our investigation particularly since Elijah's supplication for rain occurred immediately after his execution of the 450 false prophets.

Elijah was a man of God and he served his kinsman as a prophet. Taking the life of one person or the lives of 450 was not something he would do flippantly. Elijah loved his people although he had experienced much hostility from them in his career as a prophet. He chose not to exchange his faith in the LORD for popularity by circumventing justice. He endured the trial and followed God's Law.

If the LORD had concluded Elijah was not living a righteous life according to His Law his prayer would have been declared an abomination. King Solomon taught that principle in Proverbs 28:9:

> 9) One who turns his ear away from hearing the law, Even his prayer is an abomination.

God's response to Elijah's prayer for rain is evidence He perceived him as an obedient servant. The LORD not only condoned the execution of the 450 false prophets of Baal, He was pleased that justice was served by faithful Elijah.

God's presence and protection over Elijah remained throughout his life. According to 2 Kings 1 the king of Samaria, Ahaziah, was injured while in his upper room. After the king sought help from the false god, Baal-Zebub, Elijah sent him a message indicating he would die for this evil. Kings weren't too fond of receiving bad news from prophets so the king sent a captain and a company of 50 men to fetch Elijah.

They found Elijah sitting on a hill where the captain addressed him as "man of God." He then commanded Elijah to come down by the authority of the king. Elijah's interesting response is recorded in 2 Kings 1:10:

> 10) "If I am a man of God, then let fire come down from heaven and consume you and your fifty men."

That is exactly what happened. Another company was sent later and Elijah also had them consumed by the fire from heaven. The third captain demonstrated a little more humility by pleading with Elijah while on his knees to come down which spared his life and the lives of his men. It appears the LORD was still listening to His righteous prophet.

Elijah is also one of only two men who had the honor to be caught up into heaven without experiencing physical death. Enoch is the other, according to Genesis 5:23-24 and Hebrews 11:5.

After Elijah selected Elisha as his successor God ended his ministry here on earth in an extraordinary way. Elisha witnessed the entire incident which is recorded in 2 Kings 2:11-12:

> 11) Then it happened, as they continued on and talked, that suddenly a chariot of fire appeared with horses of fire, and separated the two of them; and Elijah went up by a whirlwind into heaven. 12) And Elisha saw it, and he cried out, "My father, my father, the chariot of Israel and its horseman!" So he saw him no more. And he took hold of his own clothes and tore them into two pieces.

Matthew 17:1-4 documents that Elijah later appeared with Moses and spoke with the Lord Jesus on the mount of transfiguration. This was witnessed by Jesus' closest disciples: Peter, James, and John. After considering God's work in Elijah's life while here on earth and after his transportation into heaven, it is evident that Elijah is indeed highly esteemed as a man of God by the LORD Himself.

Jesus

Our investigation of Jesus' perspective on the death penalty finally brings us to the Newer Testament. We will begin with a passage in the 20th chapter of the Gospel of Luke where we will review some pertinent guidance from our Lord Jesus on the topic of the death penalty. This passage covers events that were prior to His death, burial, and resurrection but still falls in the Dispensation of the Mosaic Law for the church was not born until Acts 2. We will initially focus our attention on Luke 20:19-25.

To preface this passage we must understand the situation in Israel at this time in history. Israel was being occupied by the Roman Empire. Although Israel had an ad-hoc type government, the nation ultimately fell under the rule of the Romans. The Jews despised the Gentile dogs that forcibly inhabited their land and now ruled over them. That sentiment also pertained to any Jew that worked for the Roman government; such as the tax collectors. Jesus was born and lived in Israel while the nation experienced this time of foreign occupation.

The chief priests and the scribes wanted to arrest Jesus but feared the reaction of the people. The plan was to trick Jesus into saying something that would get Him in trouble with the Roman governor, Pontius Pilate. Jesus' opponents knew rebellion against the Roman government would ultimately lead to His arrest and death. With that in mind they presented a loaded question to Jesus and waited for their opportunity to expose His rebellion. The question is found in Luke 20:22:

22) "Is it lawful for us to pay taxes to Caesar or not?"

Jesus, while knowing that this was a trick, answered with great authority and security. He reminded them it was Caesar's image engraved on the money. His answer is recorded in verse 25 of the same chapter:

25) And He said to them, "Render therefore to Caesar the things that are Caesar's, and to God the things that are God's."

Jesus' brilliant response was void of any evidence of treason against the Roman government. He also demonstrated His allegiance to the God of Israel. As a result, His enemies marveled at His answer and were stumped into silence. The Jews desired for Jesus to claim that the Roman government should not be obeyed for it had no authority over them. He instead explained a principle we shall witness taught again by the Apostle Paul.

Jesus admonished the people of Israel to obey the laws of their ruling government which included paying the required tax. Evidently the Jewish people could also rest assured they would not be dishonoring their LORD by supporting the Roman government through the tax system.

Jesus' confirmation that He and the rest of Israel fell under the rule of the Romans is significant. The Romans had civil laws that required the death penalty as the punishment for the violator. Crucifixion was the contemporary form of execution used by the Romans in death penalty cases. It was brutal and very tortuous. The pain inflicted on the condemned was so extreme it was beyond any description the Romans had at that time. As a result, a new word was formed based upon the word "crucifixion." We know the word as "excruciating," which literally means "out of the cross."(34)

It is recorded in John 19 that Jesus was later arrested and taken to Pontius Pilate. The Jews tried to convince Pilate that Jesus deserved to be put to death. They called for His crucifixion in John 19:6. However, Pilate indicated that he found no fault in Jesus that would require putting Him to death. The Jews then mentioned that their Law required His death because Jesus claimed to be the Son of God. This caused additional anxiety for Pilate for he feared a possible Jewish uprising. He went back to ask Jesus, "Where are you from?"

Jesus remained silent and gave no answer to Pilate. Pilate then asks the following intriguing question in verse 10:

> 10) "Are You not speaking to me? Do You not know that I have power to crucify You, and power to release You?"

What I see here is a great opportunity. Pilate claimed to have the legitimate authority to sentence a person to death as a penalty for violating the law. This was an opening for Jesus to correct any flawed perception Pilate had in reference to the government's moral right to administer capital punishment. Jesus' response is recorded in John 19:11:

> 11) "You could have no power at all against Me unless it had been given you from above. Therefore the one who delivered Me to you has the greater sin."

Jesus confirmed Pilate's claim. Pilate had the authority as a governing official. In fact, the Lord recognized that He fell under the authority of Pilate's rule. The Savior showed tremendous humility here particularly since He is a King Himself. However, He had already explained to Pilate that His Kingdom is not of this world (John 18:36). The Lord placed Himself under the authority of the temporal ruler of the land in which He lived.

Jesus taught the governor an additional lesson: Pilate's power to rule the land was ultimately given to him from God. The LORD is the One who created the governmental entity to provide stability in any land. The power needed to fulfill that function is always ordained by God. We will later see more explanation of this concept when we study the book of Romans.

Notice also that Jesus did not seize the opportunity to explicitly denounce the use of the death penalty. This would have been a great place to clear up this controversy. He didn't even address the issue of crucifixion and the brutality it involves. Jesus instead addressed Pilate's arrogance in regards to the origin of his power. The governor's power to rule and render decisions on life or death was assigned to him from God.

Jesus was eventually taken to be crucified between two others at a place called in Hebrew, Galgotha, translated as "the Place of a Skull," according to John 19:17-18. Luke 23:32-33 adds that this place was also known as Calvary and the two others to be crucified beside Jesus were criminals. I would like to draw our attention now to the conversation recorded in Luke 23:39-43.

Jesus was heavily mocked from those who stood by and watched as He hung on the cross. Eventually one of the criminals joined in the mocking by saying the following in verse 39:

39) "If you are the Christ, save Yourself and us."

The other criminal rebuked the man for not fearing God. This was evident by the man's mocking of the Christ. This was particularly inappropriate since the mocking criminal was about to die with Jesus. Even more interesting is the responding criminal's words to his belligerent accomplice about their punishment of death in verse 41:

41) "And we indeed justly, for we receive the due reward of our deeds; but this Man has done nothing wrong."

The responding convict reminded the mocker that they were being crucified justly for they had broken the law. Jesus' execution was not righteous but not because the death penalty was immoral. The Lord's punishment was unjustified because He was an innocent man. Jesus had passed the tests of His Jewish enemies and nothing could be found unrighteous about Him. His life was impeccable, void of any violations of Roman or Biblical law.

Consider the fact that Jesus was hanging between the two criminals as they had this conversation. He would have heard every word including the responding criminal's claim that their execution was just according to their deeds. Some readers of this passage may conclude Jesus was unable to respond because of the loss of blood He had already experienced. However, we know He was still conscious and coherent because of the exchange between the repentant criminal and the Lord in verses 42-43:

> 42) Then he said to Jesus, "Lord, remember me when You come into Your kingdom." 43) And Jesus said to him, "Assuredly, I say to you, today you will be with Me in Paradise."

According to verse 44 Jesus did not die for another three hours or so. We can conclude Jesus heard this conversation about the death penalty. He heard the responding criminal make the statement that their crucifixion was a fair punishment because they were guilty of violating the law of the land. The only concern was that Jesus' execution was unjust because He was blameless.

Jesus again had the opportunity to reveal truth about the government's authority to execute convicted criminals. The repentant criminal had also placed his faith in Jesus as the Christ and joined the Lord that day in Paradise. The Savior surely would have corrected this newly believing disciple's view of the death penalty if it were truly an evil act. In fact, Jesus never labeled the government's use of the death penalty as evil during His earthly ministry and His ministry took place during the time when crucifixion was the form of execution.

Finally, Jesus previously responded to accusations from some Pharisees and teachers of the Law in Matthew 15:1-6. Their claim was that Jesus' disciples were violating the traditions of the elders by not washing their hands prior to eating. Jesus rebuked His enemies for they had replaced the true commandments of God with their traditions.

In verse 4 He explicitly alluded to two commandments showing their failure to honor their parents and to administer the death penalty to the person who curses their father or mother. It is indeed an interesting notion that the Savior selected these two commands from all of the Law to expose their hypocrisy.

Dispensation of Grace

Peter

Perhaps you have remembered and taken issue with a statement made by the Apostle Peter in regards to the death penalty. The statement to which I am referring is his accusation against the Jewish leadership in reference to the crucifixion of Jesus. The apostle's allegation occurred after the birth of the church which took place in Acts 2. This passage falls in the Dispensation of Grace.

The *New King James Version Bible* utilizes the English word "murdered" in its translation of Peter's complaint. The choice of this specific and limited term may potentially cause alarm. Peter was quoted by Luke, the author of Acts, in Acts 5:30 as saying the following:

> 30) "The God of our fathers raised up Jesus whom you murdered by hanging on a tree."

100

The Greek word translated here as "murdered" is also translated as "slew" or "killed" in other English versions of the Bible. However, I am confident you will agree with me "murder" is indeed the best translation after we investigate the immediate context. If that's true, it possibly could be construed that Peter was making an absolute statement about the use of the death penalty. On the other hand, perhaps he was claiming the truth of Scripture found in Exodus 23:7:

> 7) "Keep yourself far from a false matter; do not kill the innocent and righteous. For I will not justify the wicked.

The apostle held the Jewish leadership culpable of murder since they sent Jesus, who was blameless, to be crucified based upon intentional false testimony and false accusations they brought against Him. According to Luke 23:2 Jesus' captors told Pilate the following:

> 2) "We found this fellow perverting the nation, and forbidding to pay taxes to Caesar, saying that He Himself is Christ, a King."

Jesus did indeed claim He was the Christ. However, we can ascertain these are blatantly false accusations by the Jewish leaders by reviewing Jesus' actual response to the question on paying taxes (Luke 20:19-25). The Hebrew Law found in Deuteronomy 19:15-21 is clear. Anyone who provides false testimony which sends an innocent person to their death shall also be put to death themselves. Israel's religious leadership purposely sent an innocent man to His death based upon lies and deceit.

Peter did not hold the Jewish leaders accountable for murder in regards to the two criminals who were crucified with Jesus. If the death penalty or even the brutality of crucifixion were the issue, surely Peter would have mentioned the other two persons who had suffered with the Lord. Additionally, he stated it was the Jewish leadership that murdered the Lord. The Romans were the executioners who physically placed Jesus on the cross and carried out the crucifixion. Peter never called the Romans murderers.

The apostle's immediate indictment was against the Jewish leadership who falsely accused Jesus of blasphemy and treason which sent a Holy and Righteous Man to His death. The Jews chose to have a murderer, Barabbas, released from the Roman's death row in order to have Jesus, the Author of Life, crucified in his stead (Acts 3:14-15). Therefore, Jesus' execution could legitimately be labeled a murder and the Jewish leadership would be held blameworthy for that offense.

Peter definitely had the same perspective as the Lord Jesus in regards to human government and its function in maintaining stability in the land through the administration of justice. We can observe Peter's teaching on that very subject in his first canonical epistle.

Early in 1 Peter, the apostle admonished believers in Christ to have their conduct be found honorable, even to unbelievers. This was to prevent any basis for accusation against them. Their good works would bring glory to God. Peter continued by exhorting them in respect to their relationship to the ruling king's government in 1 Peter 2:13-17:

> 13) Therefore submit yourselves to every ordinance of man for the Lord's sake, whether to the king as supreme, 14) or to the governors, as to those who are sent by him for the punishment of evildoers and for the praise of those who do good. 15) For this is the will of God, that by doing good you may put to silence the ignorance of foolish

men-16) as free, yet not using liberty as a cloak for vice,
but as bondservants of God. 17) Honor all people. Love
the brotherhood. Fear God. Honor the king.

Peter did not explicitly address the death penalty issue. He did
explain we all should voluntarily obey the laws of the land and honor
those who rule over us. We obey for "the Lord's sake." We please
the Lord by obeying the laws and ordinances of man. If we choose
not to obey we can expect the consequences legitimately assigned
to us by those who are delegated with the power to punish evildoers.

Peter did not explicitly share a perspective on the use of the
death penalty by the governing officials. On the other hand, the
Apostle Paul provided clarity on the issue through his recorded
authoritative speech in the book of Acts and his canonical writings
such as Romans.

Paul

The events of the Apostle Paul's third missionary journey are
documented in Acts 18:23-21:16. At the end of this trip the apostle
was determined to return to Jerusalem against the will of many who
loved him. Paul was well aware of the danger for there were Jews
in the holy city seeking to kill him. Acts 21:17-25:9 reveals Paul's
experience following his arrival in Jerusalem.

Paul was able to freely minister in the city until it was learned by
the Jews he had brought a Greek into the temple. As a result, he was
seized by a group of people who had intentions of killing him. Paul
was eventually rescued by Roman soldiers and centurions who were
led by a commander later identified as Claudius Lysias.

A little over forty Jewish men took an oath pledging they would
not eat until they killed Paul. They even prepared to ambush any

escort protecting the apostle in order to fulfill their objective. Their conspiracy was ultimately revealed to Commander Lysias by Paul's nephew who overheard the plan. Lysias responded by assigning even more soldiers to transport Paul to Governor Felix in Caesarea so that he might hear the accusations himself.

Felix was briefed on the case against Paul by Tertullus who spoke for the Jewish high priest Ananias, and the elders. Their accusation against Paul was that he was a plague and a creator of dissension among all the Jews throughout the world. They also charged him as a ring leader of the sect of the Nazarenes who had attempted to profane the temple.

Paul was later given his chance to explain himself before Felix. Afterward the governor refused to make a decision but instead detained Paul for two years. Governor Felix was eventually succeeded by Porcius Festus.

Festus went to Jerusalem where he heard the Jew's case against Paul. Of course the governor was familiar with the Roman law: The accused must be afforded a trial where he could face his accusers and declare his defense (Acts 25:16). He invited the Jews to travel with him to Caesarea in order to charge Paul.

When they arrived there the Jews made serious complaints against the apostle but could not prove them. Paul denied offending any law including Caesar's. As a favor to Paul's accusers, Festus asked him if he would return to Jerusalem to be judged before him there. The apostle's striking reply is recorded in Acts 25:10-11:

> 10) So Paul said, "I stand at Caesar's judgment seat, where I ought to be judged. To the Jews I have done no wrong, as you very well know. 11) "For if I am an offender, or have committed anything deserving of death, I do not object to dying; but if there is nothing in these

things of which these men accuse me, no one can deliver me to them. I appeal to Caesar."

Paul made a significant confirmation. Festus, being the governor, had the authority from Caesar himself to hear and render decisions on cases warranting death for the convicted. For this reason it was called Caesar's judgment seat. According to the apostle even his execution would be righteous if he had committed any offense against the Roman Empire deserving of death. Consequently, the government has the moral right to execute convicted violators of the law.

We can reach the same conclusion through the evidence of omission. Paul had a similar opportunity the Lord Jesus had during His personal earthly ministry. The death penalty issue was in discussion between Paul and Festus. The fact the apostle did not seize the moment to claim the death penalty was evil is certainly material.

What's more disturbing is the pagan Romans demonstrated a greater sense of urgency in preventing the death of an innocent person than were the Jews. Per Roman law it was mandatory that witnesses against the accused be present to give their testimony. While on the other hand, the Jews were looking to seize Paul and kill another innocent man in violation of their own Law which they claimed to be protecting. The apostle revealed significant evidence on Christ's perspective of the death penalty. However, he provided even more insight on the subject in his letter to the Christians in Rome.

The book of Romans is a letter from the Apostle Paul to the believers in Christ who were living in Rome. It appears the epistle was scribed for Paul by a man named Tertius, according to Romans 16:22. The estimated date the letter was written is 57 A.D. The Caesar and ruler of Rome was Nero who inflicted a brutal campaign of persecution on the church. With that in mind, I believe you will soon agree that Paul, while under the inspiration of the Holy Spirit, demonstrated tremendous humility in this narrative particularly in the text found in Romans13.

In order to give us a flow contextually, we should first observe the last eight verses of chapter 12 where Paul was instructing the believers in Rome on individual conduct toward others. He wrote the following in verses 14, 17 and 19:

14) Bless those who curse you; bless and do not curse.

17) Repay no one evil for evil.

19) Beloved, do not avenge yourselves, but rather give place to wrath; for it is written, "Vengeance is Mine, I will repay," says the Lord.

Notice these three verses deal specifically with our reaction to those who have wronged us. In Romans 12:19 Paul alluded to Deuteronomy 32:35 where God spoke of dealing with Israel's disobedience. He was teaching it's not our place to take vengeance against another person even when we've personally been offended. Paul wasn't teaching that vengeance is evil or will not eventually be accomplished. This was a reminder that it's the Lord's place to take vengeance and repay evil. The legitimate question is: How and when will the Lord repay and bring vengeance on those who do evil to others?

The question of swift justice is not solely a contemporary concern. King David conveyed a similar form of anxiety in the Psalms. For instance, David wrote the following in Psalm 37: 1-2:

1) A Psalm of David. Do not fret because of evildoers, Nor be envious of the workers of iniquity. 2) For they shall be cut down like the grass, And wither as the green herb.

Asaph also shared in Psalm 73 his perspective on the same topic as he watched the wicked prosper. He described the arrogance of those evildoers as they mocked the LORD by questioning God's knowledge of their evil activities. Notice the psalmist's words in verse 11:

11) And they say, "How does God know? And is there knowledge in the Most High?"

People have always struggled with watching evil seemingly go without consequence. The challenge is to remain calm, wait, and resist in taking vengeance especially when the offense is committed against us personally. Those who believe in Christ are not exempt from such fears.

Although we know God will one day exact eternal judgment, we wonder if He also holds individuals temporally accountable for their actions. I believe David was teaching the LORD deals with evildoers temporally. In other words, those who offend the laws of society will experience judgment from God in the present. The Apostle Paul answered this valid concern in Romans 13:1-4:

1) Let every soul be subject to the governing authorities. For there is no authority except from God, and the authorities that exist are appointed by God. 2) Therefore whoever resists the authority resists the ordinance of God, and those who resist will bring judgment on themselves. 3) For rulers are not a terror to good works, but to evil. Do you want to be unafraid of the authority? Do what is good, and you will have praise from the same. 4) For he is God's minister to you for good. But if you do evil, be

afraid; for he does not bear the sword in vain; for he is God's minister, an avenger to execute wrath on him who practices evil.

Even while keenly aware of Rome's hate for the church, Paul still didn't hesitate to exhort the Christians of their responsibility to obey the government that ruled over them. In fact, one could say it was even a warning. The apostle wrote the following in Romans 13:1:

1) Let every soul be subject to the governing authorities. For there is no authority except from God, and the authorities that exist are appointed by God.

Paul, in his authority as an apostle, commanded that "every" person is to submit to the rule of their government. Paul said each citizen should obey the civil laws although his guidance was never directed toward unbelievers. He was in essence informing the Christians they are not exempt. They lived in the land ruled by Rome so they were to obey the laws established by the Roman government.

Interestingly, Paul did not explicitly speak of the Roman government. As a result we can conclude that every Christian is commanded to abide by their ruling authority regardless of which specific administration that may be.

Paul then used the word "for" in verse 1b in order to make a connection with verse 1a. He instructed that the authority to which the believer submits is essentially from God Himself. The origin of the government's power is not from itself. This sounds similar to the principle taught during the conversation Jesus had with Pontius Pilate in John 19:10-11.

Paul further explained in verse 1c the ruling authorities are personally appointed by God. This is very important as we continue with verse 2:

2) Therefore whoever resists the authority resists the ordinance of God, and those who resist will bring judgment on themselves.

Paul began with "therefore" in verse 2 to make the following point: Since the authority of the human government comes from God, we essentially resist the LORD when we disobey the law of the land. Is Paul teaching that I am breaking the law of the land and ultimately sinning against God if I drive 65 mph in a 55 mph roadway zone? Obviously the answer is yes.

Of course this principle is not exclusively for believers in Christ. All persons living under the authorities' rule will experience the same potential consequences for violating the law. The comprehension of this principle is especially important for any Christian who mistakenly trusts they will escape the government's response to their rebellion based solely upon their relationship with Christ.

Paul warned we will bring judgment upon ourselves if we choose to break the law. He was admonishing Christians in Rome who chose to resist the pagan and hostile Roman government. God would not protect them from the human authorities when they were judged and condemned for their actions. In fact, I believe it's accurate to conclude God is even stricter on believers because we are His children. Regardless, anyone who opts to offend the law of the land will be reprimanded by the LORD through the agency of the human penal system. The apostle continues with the following in Romans 12:3:

3) For rulers are not a terror to good works, but to evil. Do you want to be unafraid of the authority? Do what is good, and you will have praise from the same.

Paul revealed that terror is the objective of the rulers' punishment and judgment. This reminds me of the "hear and fear" reaction God intended to produce among the people of Israel when harsh consequences were administered. The LORD knows people need a healthy fear of the authorities. Terror acts as a form of deterrence from future lawlessness. This principle definitely worked for me when my teachers would set a paddle on their desk in view of the entire class. My buttocks would hurt while merely looking at it. Fear of that paddling kept me from committing many types of infractions in school.

Paul clarified the function of the government is to strike fear into the hearts of a targeted group, those who are doing evil. In the same breath, Paul offered an alternative for anyone thinking of rebellion against the government: Do that which is good and you will have nothing to fear.

Paul also explained that the authority has a sense of appreciation. Those who are doing good in the land don't need to be afraid. On the contrary, they can even expect praise from their leaders. Just a reminder, Peter described the same principle in 1 Peter 2:14. Now, before we move to Romans 13:4 we should review verses 1-3.

Paul admonished that all people are to submit to their government. The LORD established the governmental entity and its authority originates from Him. For this reason, we resist God when we rebel against the government. We can expect temporal judicial reprimand when we commit evil acts. This judgment is ultimately from God through the governmental institution. His intention of using temporal judgment through the governing authority is to bring terror upon those who do evil in the land. Those who are doing "good" should not fear but instead can expect praise from their rulers.

As we now move to verse 4 consider Paul's instruction in Romans 12 in regards to vengeance. He reminded the individual not to seek and execute it for themselves. We are not to repay evil for evil for it's the Lord's place to exact vengeance in the world. If the Lord demanded vengeance is His, we can be confident He will achieve it. This is why Romans 13:4 is so crucial. Let's start by studying the following in verse 4a:

4a) For he is God's minister to you for good.

Paul labeled "he" as a minister of God. Who is he? Of course we can contextually determine "he" is none other than the governmental authority. Paul is teaching that the ruling institution is a minister of God. The term "minister" typically leads one to envision a pastor who performs his duties by serving his congregation as he leads them and teaches them in the matters of their relationship with God. The minister is used by God for the benefit of people.

The Greek term translated as "minister" in this verse is διάκονος (*diakonos*). It has also been translated in other areas of the Newer Testament as "servant," "attendant," and "deacon."(35) A servant or minister of God assists in accomplishing God's purposes. The LORD loves people and He's passionate in doing good to all who are created in His image. According to Paul God is blessing all citizens of the world via His servant, human government.

It may seem somewhat awkward that a pagan government, like that in Rome, could be used by God as a minister. Yet the LORD is not limited to working through those who love Him to fulfill His goals. He has historically used pagan countries and nations to achieve His objectives particularly while He dealt with Israel's dis-obedience. God even titled a pagan ruler, Cyrus, as His "anointed" because God had a special mission for him to subdue and humble the nations (Isaiah 44:28-45:1). The LORD used a demon with the intention of keeping Paul humble when the demonic enemy would have loved for the apostle to become proud about his visit to Paradise (2 Corinthians 12: 2-7). God is infinite. He can utilize anyone, even those who shake their fist in defiance at Him, in order to accomplish His good pleasure.

We also observe this ministry is for the good of all people, even those who don't believe in Him. This is often called by theologians as God's "Common Grace." This is grace God bestows to all people regardless of their relationship to Him. Other examples of His common grace are His rising of the sun and His pouring of rain on the just and the unjust (Matthew 5:45).

Similar to the life which the sun and the rain sustain, people can experience security and order through the ministry provided by the rulers of their land. Paul explained how this security will be achieved in the rest of verse 4:

> 4) For he is God's minister to you for good. But if you do evil, be afraid; for he does not bear the sword in vain; for he is God's minister, an avenger to execute wrath on him who practices evil.

Paul again emphasized the exhortation to those who choose to resist the authority and break the law. They should be afraid because the government does not bear the sword in vain. On the contrary, the earthly rulers wield this weapon for a purpose. Notice Paul did not say he carries the shield. A shield may seem to be a better word picture since the government provides security and protects its population. The apostle chose the word "sword" which is an instrument of killing and death. The minister does not bear the sword in vain because he will righteously employ this lethal implement and take the lives of those who resist his authority.

It's interesting how Paul established the nobility of this potentially controversial idea of the government's right to administer the death penalty. He places the phrase "for he is God's minister" before and after revealing the authority's function of bearing the sword. It appears Paul was just reiterating the fact that this task of the earthly rulers is indeed a good service provided from God to all people.

Paul finished verse 4 by calling the government an avenger. The Greek word here is ἔκδικος (*Ekdikos*). In *An Expository Dictionary of New Testament Words*, W.E. Vine wrote, "Ekdikos, primarily, without law, then, one who exacts a penalty from a person, an avenger, a punisher, is used in Romans13:4 of a civil authority in the discharge of his function of executing wrath on the evildoer."(36) This avenger has a purpose to execute wrath on him who practices evil.

The Greek term translated to vengeance is very similar to Ekdikos. It is ἐκδίκησις (*Ekdikesis*). An interesting observation is the Greek root δικα (*dike*) is found in ἐκδίκησις (*Ekdikesis*). The word δικα (*dike*) is commonly found in Greek words containing the meaning of justice or just conduct. It's also found in Greek words meaning to justify or to declare righteous.

Ekdikesis, vengeance, is the word used in Romans 12:19. It means "that which proceeds from justice, not, as often with human vengeance, out of a sense of injury or merely out of a feeling of indignation."(37) This vengeance sought by God through the governing authorities is righteous and pure and it encompasses true justice.

The word "wrath" in verse 4 is significant in regards to interpreting the time frame of God's judgment. This word is derived from the Greek term ὀργὴν (*orge*). Wrath carries the meaning of anger and it is found 12 times in the book of Romans. Throughout its uses in Paul's epistle, it is never found in contexts where ὀργὴν (*orge*) should be interpreted as meaning the "eternal" wrath of God experienced by those who go to hell. It actually should be contextually interpreted in each instance as the "temporal" wrath of God exacted during the human life experience. (38) We can easily interpret wrath this way in this context of Romans 13. This wrath will be executed by the governing authorities who exist now in the temporal realm. It will be experienced in the present.

There is also an interesting observation of omission. Paul left out any explicit violations that warrant the use of the death penalty. The determination of which offense warrants capital punishment is evidently left to the prerogative of each individual government. Paul did not set a restriction of the death penalty for those convicted of murder only. This should be no surprise after we studied the multiple violations in the Hebrew Law that were punishable by death.

The criminals that were crucified with Jesus were not murderers. They were called thieves or robbers. If a government assigns the death penalty for the offense of spitting on the sidewalk, it would behoove the citizen of that land to refrain from committing that offense.

Paul confirmed several things about the human governmental institution. It is established by God and its authority is from Him. Those who break the laws of the land resist their rulers and ultimately sin against the LORD. God has not abdicated His responsibility to avenge for rebellion against Himself but has delegated the authority to the human governments to execute His and their wrath through penal sentencing on those who practice evil. The appointed administration has the moral right to execute the death penalty on the individual who defies its ruling authority through civil disobedience. The exacted justice will provide stability in the land by detouring future acts of evil through fear of harsh consequences. This is considered the ministry of the government to the people of all nations for good which is based upon God's common grace. Therefore, when we witness the execution of a convicted criminal, we can justifiably declare, "it is good."

I believe our study so far has shown a clear and consistent perspective conveyed from the Scriptures on the subject of the death penalty. Again, since the Bible is considered the Word of God, we can confidently declare this is also the perspective of Christ. It's apparent that God's command is that the death penalty is righteous and a fitting punishment especially for those who murder.

Is the responsibility of the governmental authority to suppress evil with the sword restricted to the death penalty? Are the lives of violent offenders secure until the day they might be executed? We'll set out to answer these legitimate questions as we now seek Christ's perspective on the use of deadly force. We shall again start our investigation in the earlier dispensations to reveal the same consistency of the Scriptures in regards to the use of deadly force by the citizen in self-defense.

9

SELF-DEFENSE

American hearts were shattered on December 14, 2012, when 20 elementary school children and six adults were slaughtered by a gunman at the Sandy Hook Elementary School in Newtown, Connecticut. The murderer ended the rampage when he committed suicide with a self-inflicted gunshot wound to the head. The carnage of the scene which included the corpses of so many children was too much to bear for even hardened SWAT team members and veteran detectives.

The sting of Sandy Hook immediately ignited debate on arming school teachers for defense of themselves and our children. Evidently an unarmed staff member attempted to stop the killing but lost her life in the effort. A related discussion formed on Facebook based upon a posted comment suggesting if the Sandy Hook teachers were armed they could have shot the suspect. One of the persons in the conversation responded: "I don't think that's what Jesus would do!"

Of course the statement's implication is that killing in self-defense is "anti-Christ" or immoral. Similar to the popular "What Would Jesus Do" (WWJD) acronym, it also conveys an assumption that Jesus is in heaven doing nothing. According to the Scriptures the Spirit of Christ is still presently working through individual believers who form the universal church. The Lord is currently showcasing His character to the world through those believers who yield to His Spirit and His Word.

With that in mind, can the believer in Christ kill in self-defense and accurately claim to be in fellowship with Him? Does the Lord Jesus actually expect the folk of any land to passively watch while such heinous violence is perpetrated on fellow citizens? We shall now search the sacred writings to find Jesus' consistent view on the topic of deadly force and killing in self-defense. We shall begin our examination by returning to the book of Genesis.

Dispensation of Conscience or Self-Determination

God

We'll start by examining Genesis 3:22-24. The sin of Adam and Eve had occurred and as a result they possessed the knowledge of good and evil which is why this portion of Scripture falls in the Dispensation of Conscience or Self-Determination. The LORD demonstrated His grace by clothing the couple with tunics He made from animal skin. In verses 22-23 He revealed a concern that Adam and Eve were vulnerable to a new danger because of their fallen state. If the couple were to eat from the tree of life, which was also in the garden, they would live physically forever in that condition of being separated from God. Therefore, He sent them out of the garden of Eden to till the ground from which they were taken. In order to prevent any entrance back into the garden and ultimately access to the tree of life, God responded with the following action recorded in verse 24:

117

24) So, He drove out the man; and He placed cherubim at the east of the garden of Eden, and a flaming sword which turned every way, to guard the way to the tree of life.

The LORD posted a sentry of angels at the garden's entrance with a valid purpose. God's sense of urgency for the couple's protection was made evident by placing a flaming sword at the entrance as well. The sword was not only flaming, it was mobile. This weapon would not fall to evasive maneuvers by anyone seeking to enter the garden. The LORD's choice of weapon, the sword, is even more intriguing.

As we discussed earlier in Chapter Eight the sword has the purpose of striking and killing. An interesting additional observation is this blade was not being controlled by the guarding angels. It appears to be controlled by the Holy Spirit, the Spirit of Christ. The LORD was wielding this weapon and He surely was not bearing it in vain. He would fight and kill anyone who attempted to pass His gauntlet.

God's goodness is confirmed by His resolve to protect man from increasing his suffering by consuming from the tree of life. Personally I find it fascinating God would exhibit His love and mercy by killing the potential trespasser in order to protect the same person's life. Although this is a very unique and unorthodox situation, God demonstrated the righteousness of using deadly force in self-defense.

Dispensation of the Mosaic Law

Moses

The Scripture in the book of Exodus associated with the use of deadly force in self-defense is particularly interesting to me. The

118

grounds for my interest will be revealed later as we move through this study of Exodus 22. This specific portion of the Mosaic Law covers the civil laws for the nation of Israel. Exodus 22:2-3a reads:

> 2) "If the thief is found breaking in, and he is struck so that he dies, there shall be no guilt for his bloodshed. 3a) "If the sun has risen on him, there shall be guilt for his bloodshed.

According to the Texas Penal Code the elements of this offense described above are comparable to the offense of Burglary. This decree from the LORD to the children of Israel basically states the thief who broke into any establishment during the nighttime hours had risked his own life. It was considered justifiable homicide if the thief was killed during a burglary that occurred while the sun was not shining. Yet, the Spirit of Christ didn't lead Moses to elaborate on His motive for restricting the use of deadly force to the dark hours. In other words, why the nighttime only?

Apparently there's something about the commission of this type of crime in the dark hours that, in the eyes of God, enhances either the violent nature of the offense or the fear experienced by the victim. Perhaps the LORD was considering that the entire family is more likely to be in the targeted residence at that time placing even more persons in panic and danger. Although God's specific purpose for this rule is not offered, this Scripture plainly teaches the use of deadly force leading to the death of the intruder in this instance was deemed righteous.

There is also an interesting observation of omission. The passage doesn't mention a requirement to prove the thief was armed during the commission of the burglary. The subject who killed the offender was not required to produce evidence the suspect entered the structure armed in order to justify the use of deadly force. According to verse 3a there was one stipulation. If the incident occurred after the sun broke the horizon, there would be judicial consequences for the person who killed the offender. The thief caught in the act during the day was to be arrested and forced to pay restitution (Exodus 22:3b-4).

My personal interest in this portion of Scripture is based upon its self-defense standard. A similar principle is located in the Texas Penal Code. As I explained in Chapter Five of this book, Chapter 9 of the Texas Penal Code encompasses the rules for the justified uses of force and deadly force in the State of Texas. Section 9.42 gives guidance on the legal use of deadly force during the act of protecting property.

Basically, section 9.42(A) explains that one is justified in using deadly force during the nighttime hours in order to prevent another from committing theft and criminal mischief (vandalism). 9.42(B) continues by clarifying that deadly force is also justified during the nighttime hours when one is attempting to prevent the suspect from escaping with the property after committing theft.

The rest of the section adds a condition. The one using deadly force must have reasonably believed the land or property could not have been protected by any other means or the use of force, other than deadly force, would have placed the actor or another in substantial risk of death or serious bodily injury.(39)

There is definitely something about the dark that enhances our fear and sense of danger. Imagine waking up in your home at 3:00 am and finding a burglar carrying your flat screen television through the living room. You would probably agree that would be somewhat more frightening than for the same to occur at 3:00 pm.

The victim's fear of serious bodily injury or death is naturally more intense in the dark.

The other consideration for nighttime burglary is reduced visibility. The distortion of the victim's sight is crucial in this context. The inability to see in the dark alone causes anxiety. The stress would be substantially increased because the victim is unable to determine whether or not the offender is armed.

It's possible the LORD was teaching that the nighttime victim could legitimately assume the offender possessed a weapon and intended to cause injury, even serious bodily injury or death, during the commission of the burglary. Therefore the victim was permitted to use deadly force to protect himself, his family, and his property. This may explain why the LORD commanded the arrest of the daytime burglar since the ability to confirm the presence of weapons would be improved.

In the Ryrie Study Bible Dr. Charles Ryrie gives his interpretation of Exodus 22:2-3 as the following: "The meaning is this: killing a thief who was digging through a wall after dark was justifiable homicide, but to do so in daylight subjected the householder to revenge by the thief's next of kin."(40) That next of kin would be the burglar's "avenger of blood" we observed in Numbers 35.

The commentators of the *Nelson Study Bible New King James Version* give a slightly different opinion of the meaning of the phrase "if the sun has risen on him." According to these scholars, the phrase emphasizes when in the process of the offense the thief is caught rather than the hour. The commentary reads: "to strike the thief after the act would be considered inappropriate use of force."(41) In other words, the urgency of self defense, of person or property, was lost if the thief was caught after the offense was committed.

Regardless of which interpretation of the phrase "if the sun has risen on him" we embrace, the overall message is explicitly clear. This Mosaic Law precept provided the children of Israel with the standard and moral support to protect themselves and their property. The Holy Spirit, the Spirit of Christ, led Moses to speak and document the Law. The LORD God permitted His chosen national people to use deadly force in the context of self-defense. A godly leader named Nehemiah demonstrated his faith in this truth later in Israel's history.

Nehemiah

I explained earlier that the nation of Israel split into two kingdoms around 931 BC., the northern kingdom of Israel and the southern kingdom of Judah. Both kingdoms were eventually found to be disobedient to God so He disciplined them by way of exile. Israel was taken first into captivity by the Assyrians in 722 B.C. Judah was later overtaken by the Babylonian empire in 605 B.C. which was followed by the destruction of Jerusalem and the temple in 586 B.C. The Babylonians were ultimately defeated by the Medes and Persians later in history.

Nehemiah was a faithful Jewish man living in the Persian Empire in the middle of the 5th century B.C. He was assigned as the cupbearer to the Persian king, Artaxerxes. Evidently Nehemiah was faithful to Artaxerxes which resulted in a healthy relationship with the king. Nehemiah received bad news about his homeland; specifically that Jerusalem was in shambles. The city's protective wall was completely broken down and the gates were on fire. The remnant of Jews who had returned to Jerusalem from Babylon was in great distress while living without the protection of the wall.

Nehemiah's face didn't hide his emotions well from the king. Artaxerxes confronted the cupbearer about his sad expression. Nehemiah uttered a quick prayer to the LORD then explained to the king the state of affairs in Jerusalem. He asked the king for permission to go back to Jerusalem to rebuild. Artaxerxes consented and gave Nehemiah the command to travel to the holy city and begin building the wall. It is estimated the king's directive was given on Nisan 1, 444 B.C. The Jewish month Nisan usually coincides with March and April.

Nehemiah journeyed back to Jerusalem and began to lead the restoration of the wall. King Artaxerxes even aided in the mission by providing materials for the project. However, there were some who inhabited the area surrounding the holy city who objected to the restoration of Jerusalem. The main enemies of Judah and their rebuilding operation were Sanballat the Horonite, the Ammonite official, Tobiah, and many others including the Arabs and the Ashdodites. Notice the description of the situation provided in Nehemiah 4:6-8:

> 6) So we built the wall, and the entire wall was joined together up to the half of its height, for the people had a mind to work. 7) Now it happened, when Sanballat, Tobiah, the Arabs, the Ammonites, and the Ashdodites heard that the walls of Jerusalem were being restored and the gaps were beginning to be closed, that they became very angry, 8) and all of them conspired together to come and attack Jerusalem and create confusion.

Judah's enemies also conveyed their plan of attack for stopping the project which is recorded in verse 11:

> 11) And our adversaries said, "They will never know nor see anything, till we come into their midst and kill them and cause the work to cease."

Israel's adversaries were motivated and they despised the notion of the nation's permanent presence in the land. As a result their plan evolved beyond conventional violence. According to verse 12 the Jews who were living near Nehemiah's enemies were cleverly deployed to use psychological warfare in order to discourage the building effort:

> 12) So it was, when the Jews who dwelt near them came, that they told us ten times, "From whatever place you turn, they will be upon us."

Nehemiah had demonstrated a crucial facet of his character up to this point. He was a leader. This faithful Jewish man refused to respond to the threats of violence and death by the enemy. He knew the completion of the wall was paramount to the future of his people and the city of Jerusalem. This great leader responded with action found in Nehemiah 4:13-14:

> 13) Therefore I positioned men behind the lower parts of the wall, at the openings; and I set the people according to their families, with their swords, their spears, and their bows. 14) And I looked, and arose and said to the nobles, to the leaders, and to the rest of the people, "Do not be afraid of them. Remember the Lord, great and awesome, and fight for your brethren, your sons, your daughters, your wives, and your houses."

Since there was no official army to summon for the protection of the people and the building project, Nehemiah called on the men, the nobles, and the officials, to take up arms and stand their ground. They were encouraged to fight their fear by remembering the Lord. Nehemiah not only encouraged each man to guard his fellow countrymen, he also emphasized the personal aspect of this mission by appealing to the protection of their own families and property. Ultimately this man of God commanded his people to arm themselves with swords, spears, and bows with the intent of using deadly force in self-defense.

Nehemiah continued the armed watch throughout the building construction process. He had half of the workers building while the other half carried weapons and wore armor. Nehemiah also noticed the workers were a little scattered while the work was commencing so he devised a plan that is found in Nehemiah 4:20:

> 20) "whenever you hear the sound of the trumpet, rally to us there. Our God will fight for us."

Nehemiah was not insinuating that Israel could remain idle and their enemies would be destroyed. If the trumpet was sounded the people were required to bear their weapons and fight to protect themselves. Their God would be with them and that fact should give them courage while they battled in self-defense. The threat of deadly force deterred any attacks from Nehemiah's foes that would have disrupted the building process. According to Nehemiah 6:15-16, the wall was finished in just 52 days which caused their enemies to be disheartened for even they perceived that the work was done by God.

Jesus

The Lord Jesus explicitly revealed His perspective on the use of deadly force in self-defense in Luke 22:35-38. It is necessary to first study a passage of Scripture in Luke 10 which contains events that occurred in the earlier stages of Jesus' earthly ministry. Again this portion of Scripture falls in the Dispensation of the Mosaic Law since the birth of the church does not occur until Pentecost which is documented in Acts 2.

According to Luke 10:1 Jesus chose 70 more disciples and sent them, two by two, into all of the cities before Him. Their mission was simple. Jesus knew there were many people ready to hear and except the message of His arrival as Messiah. His disciples were to go out and preach that the kingdom of God had come near to them (Luke 10:9). The interesting concept related to our study is located in Luke 10:3-4. First, observe what Jesus said in verse 3:

> 3) "Go your way; behold, I send you out as lambs among wolves."

This is a very interesting choice of words the Savior used to describe the two groups of people. How are lambs among wolves? They are completely vulnerable to these dangerous and violent predators. Wolves desire to attack lambs and devour them. In addition, lambs bring nothing to the confrontation that will aid them in protecting themselves from an assault.

Lambs are utterly dependent upon another, a shepherd, to provide them with protection and safety. They also are completely opposite of the wolves. Lambs are soft and cuddly. They can even be handled as a personal pet. Wolves, on the other hand, are too ferocious to be controlled and maintained in such a way.

Jesus explained why the disciples would be so vulnerable in verse 4:

> 4) "Carry neither money bag, knapsack, or sandals; and greet no one along the road."

The Lord expected his missionaries to trust in Him for their needed provisions while He was still carrying on His earthly ministry. He sent them into the world completely dependent on what was supplied by those who accepted their message. They were to take nothing but the clothes on their backs. They evidently traveled unarmed. Perhaps this is why He commanded them to greet no one along the road. Therefore, they were also relying on the Lord to provide for their physical protection while they were ministering empty-handed. Our understanding of this passage is a crucial building block to reaching an accurate interpretation of Jesus' perspective in Luke 22.

Luke 22:35-38 covers the closing stages of Jesus' personal earthly ministry. Verse 39 begins with the scene on the Mount of Olives where Jesus was eventually arrested in the garden of Gethsemane prior to His crucifixion. In verses 35-38, Jesus again gave guidance to His disciples on items they should carry as they embarked into the world for the ministry:

> 35) And He said to them, "When I sent you without money bag, knapsack, and sandals, did you lack anything?" So they said, "Nothing." 36) Then He said to them, "But now, he who has no money bag, let him take it, and likewise a knapsack; and he who has no sword, let him sell his garment and buy one. 37) "For I say to you that this which is written must still be accomplished in Me: 'And He was numbered with the transgressors.' For the things concerning Me have an end." 38) So they said, "Lord, look, here are two swords." And He said to them, "It is enough."

The fact Jesus did not change the descriptions of those in the world is indeed interesting. The disciples would still be entering areas where the wolves were prowling. Jesus took the time to remind them He was worthy of their trust. They had gone into the world earlier as sheep among the wolves and He came through for them.

They lacked nothing during that adventure. However, Jesus used two key words in verse 36a, "But now." This is an indication Jesus is about to give instructions in contrast to what He gave earlier in His ministry.

In verse 36 Jesus told His disciples to carry those things He had previously required they leave behind. He actually added a new item for the packing list. In verse 36c, the Lord urged the disciple who had no sword to sell his garment in order to buy one. Jesus made this significant point: Sell the clothing that will keep you warm to pay for the sword that may save your life.

Jesus' response at the end of verse 38, "It is enough," provides even more evidence that He condoned the carrying of weapons by His disciples. Why would Jesus now prepare the disciples to go into the world self-sufficient in supplies and bearing weapons? Luke 22:37 gives us some of the answer. The verse begins with the word "for." This is an alert of an approaching explanation of what was just previously said. Verse 37 reads:

> 37) "For I say to you that this which is written must still be accomplished in Me: 'And He was numbered with the transgressors.' For the things concerning Me have an end."

The Hebrew Scriptures were to be fulfilled in regards to Jesus' arrest and atoning death. As a result they would soon experience some violence and hostility. Jesus was enabling the disciples to protect themselves. This is why Jesus rebuked Peter for protecting the Savior in the garden of Gethsemane when he cut off Malchus' ear (John 18:10). I will cover that situation in the next chapter on Deadly Force in Policing and War.

The Lord also knew He would soon no longer physically be with His disciples. Evidently the disciples were covered with a supernatural protection while the Savior was still with them and His personal earthly ministry was active. Since He was about to leave them when He went to the cross, they would later be vulnerable to the violent world.

A concern of contradiction may develop based upon a statement Jesus made which is found in the book of Matthew. This particular comment is located in the section of Scripture called the Sermon on the Mount. According to Matthew 5:38-42 Jesus said the following:

> 38) "You have heard that it was said, 'An eye for an eye and a tooth for a tooth.' 39) "But I tell you not to resist an evil person. But whoever slaps you on your right cheek, turn the other to him also. 40) "If anyone wants to sue you and take away your tunic, let him have your cloak also. 41) "And whoever compels you to go one mile, go with him two. 42) "Give to him who asks you, and from him who wants to borrow from you do not turn away."

Jesus was obviously using hyperbole or exaggerated language in this context to drive home His points. For instance, to give your money to anyone who asks would possibly drain your resources making it impossible to take care of your family. The Apostle Paul said the person who fails to provide for his household has denied the faith and is worse than an unbeliever (1Timothy 5:8).

In verses 38-39 Jesus warned against the misuse of the Scriptures in an attempt to justify retaliation. The "eye for an eye and tooth for a tooth" principle is found in the Mosaic Law. However, it was specifically for the determination of fair punishment by judges, not the individual victim (Exodus 21:24-25; Leviticus 24:20, Deuteronomy 19:21). The victim was not permitted to resort to "street justice" or retaliation. Apparently Jesus' audience was abusing the Scripture in order to call their retaliatory acts righteous. The Savior was evidently using the hyperbolic language of "turn the other cheek" to strengthen His rebuke of their vengeful responses to previously experienced aggression.

The Lord's desire to arm his disciples for their self-defense is not in contradiction to His teaching in Matthew. Jesus should never be accused of being irrational or impractical. He was obviously mindful to the dangers of the world and it would be foolish for the disciples to travel without some means of protecting themselves. The command to carry swords would imply they had the Lord's blessing to use those weapons and kill in self-defense.

Therefore, take courage, my brothers and sisters, you who have taken the initiative to train and earn a concealed handgun license or master a martial art in edged weapons. The Lord Jesus has not called you to be floor mats to evil men who would do harm to you or your loved ones. Rest assured, you have the option to bear a weapon and use it to fight and kill, if need be, in self-defense from any aggressive action. Most importantly, you may do so in complete fellowship with the Savior.

I am confident many of you have learned something new and extraordinary about Jesus Christ after reading this chapter. I would contribute the surprised enlightenment mostly to a previously formed weak and passive image of Jesus that false teachers and the world have suggested of Him. In the next chapter we shall search the Word of God to find Christ's view on killing by those who serve as field agents of the government, such as military personnel and law enforcement.

10

POLICING AND WAR

A pril 1, 2011, was an exciting day in my life. I was blessed to attend my son's graduation from the United States Marine Corps basic training at the Marine Corps Recruitment Depot in San Diego, California. I sat in the stands and watched as 403 proud, new Marines and their remarkable Drill Instructors marched onto the hallowed parade deck demonstrating their dedication and professionalism. I also considered the many souls that had passed in review during this very ceremony in the history of the Marines which made this a highly memorable event for me.

Although these young Marines would still be attending more training prior to reaching their units, we were witnessing the finished product of a great transformation. These men were not the same persons they were when they arrived here three months earlier. The Drill Instructors had taken these young recruits through some of the toughest basic military training in the world. They were now Marines trained to fight and kill the enemy. They had become warriors to the core of their souls because nothing less is accepted by the United States Marines.

As I gazed into the sea of Marines on that parade deck, I began to ponder. I was sure each one of these 403 young men would be willing to accept any mission given to them. I had no doubt they would pull the trigger on their M-16 rifle sending lead down range on the enemy or thrusting their blade into the heart of any adversary when the circumstances demanded it. Ultimately they could and would kill in the defense of their country and any others needing their help. That's how confident I am in the Marine Corps training and the highly-motivated soldiers they produce.

A concern surfaced in my heart as I sat in those bleachers, similar to what I've experienced while watching new police officers celebrate their academy graduation. I asked myself, "Which of those new Marines are struggling within their hearts to justify killing in battle?" I thought of those who were Christians but didn't have a clear understanding on what the Bible teaches on the subject of deadly force. They could possibly be relying on their own opinions or that of others which could be very dangerous spiritually as well as physically.

If it's personally important to the soldier/police officer that God approves of their actions in battle, but they don't know the Scriptural truth of the matter, then they may hesitate to kill. Any warrior knows hesitation can be detrimental to one's health during combat. There is also the concern of how the Christian professional warrior will respond after killing another person. They must process the event in a healthy way or their ability to fulfill their soldiering duties, which will quite possibly demand they kill again, may be hindered.

It may seem prudent at this time to disclose the life experiences of the famous World War 1 U.S. Army soldier, Sgt. Alvin York. Sgt. York was a Christian who had struggled with killing but eventually received some wise Biblical counsel and became a highly decorated soldier. Sgt. York was even awarded the Medal of Honor due to his actions in battle which has resulted in books and movies covering his amazing military career.(42)

However, I believe it's more appropriate to share my personal experience which I believe will aid in conveying my motive and passion for teaching the truth taught by the Scriptures on this subject. I promised earlier to share my personal struggle with killing prior to that winter night in 1999. So, here is my story.

I received my congressional commission as a U.S. Regular Army 2nd Lieutenant in May, 1989. I was waiting to start my active duty career which would begin in January, 1990 at Fort Rucker, Alabama. I was eager to start my Aviation Officer Basic Course then move on to the U.S Army's Initial Entry Rotary Wing helicopter flight school. I had worked very hard to be accepted into the Aviation branch of the U.S. Army but I had one more semester of college to finish prior to my departure.

While I waited to leave for Alabama, I worked on completing my student teaching requirement then took on another job. During this period of time I was approached at work by a group of people carrying Bibles. We started a conversation which led to a discussion about my future career as a soldier in the Army. The group insinuated that I could not be a "real Christian" and a soldier at the same time. In other words, I would be sinning against God if I chose to be a professional soldier. Of course they quoted Scripture in defense of their claim.

I was a Christian at the time of this encounter but my knowledge of the Scriptures was sadly lacking. Regardless, I was still concerned I was about to enter into a career that inherently was unacceptable to God. Of course I was cited Scripture like, "thou shall not kill!" As I stated earlier, it's my experience this commandment from Exodus 20:13 is a favorite for those teaching this concept. The problem was I could not make an argument against their case. I was only a few months away from beginning my tour of duty as an U.S. Army Officer and now I had many questions about its legitimacy. Ultimately I was concerned I might be willfully committing sin against God if I were to kill another human being during the commission of my duty as a soldier.

I finally entered my training and finished flight school in January, 1991. I eventually was assigned to an Aviation unit at Fort Hood, Texas. When I arrived at my new unit, I still had not adequately answered the question of whether I could kill the enemy and remain in good standing with my Savior. After being at Fort Hood for a few months I decided to visit our Battalion Chaplain. God's plan had landed me in the perfect unit for answering some of my questions.

I discovered our Chaplain was one of only eleven Jewish Chaplains in the U.S. Army at the time. My meeting with the Rabbi proved to be very beneficial for he was able to teach me the more accurate translations of some of the Hebrew Scriptures. It helped me tremendously to hear that his understanding of Exodus 20:13 was "thou shall not murder." Although this was a significant leap for me, I still had much to learn in regards to what the entire Bible taught on the subject.

I exited my active duty service in January, 1993. I moved back to my home town, Wichita Falls, Texas, and was accepted that same year into the Basic Police Academy of the local police department. My future wife and I also found a sound Bible-teaching church. As a result, I became more diligent in cultivating my personal relationship with Christ which demanded time in His Word. Because the potential demand of killing another individual in combat was just as a real as a police officer, I naturally pursued Christ's "consistent" perspective on the topic.

I did not use deadly force during my time as a soldier. As you already know, that would soon change for me during my new career as a police officer. However, I was not the same person in regards to spiritual preparedness. I had been transformed from the state of uncertainty and confusion to one of confidence. Jesus' perspective of my duties as a professional warrior was no longer in question.

As a result, I boldly entered the hostile Area of Operation that night of January 10, 1999, and killed in the line of duty. I mentally processed that experience through my Scriptural grid resulting in a clear conscience. My spiritual assurance of my duties proved to be crucial because I used deadly force again during another SWAT operation just a few years later.

Our communities and nations are utterly dependent on their armed guardians and their level of readiness in every respect. Therefore, my motive for revealing the Scriptural truth on the matter of killing should be easily recognizable. I wouldn't wish the tension I experienced as a Christian warrior upon any soldier or law enforcement officer. My goal is to provide the Biblical evidence and training that will hopefully supply the same confidence I now posses.

In order to remain consistent, we shall utilize the same dispensational format to now investigate the Savior's view on the use of deadly force in the contexts of policing and war. We will begin our search by studying Scripture located in the Dispensation of Promise or Patriarchal Rule where the Spirit of Christ revealed the life experiences of a man named Abram.

Dispensation of Promise or Patriarchal Rule

Abram

Genesis 14 reveals a situation involving a man named Abram whose name was later changed to Abraham. He was called by God to leave his homeland and move to an area the LORD would later show him. In Genesis 12:1-3 the Lord disclosed His plan for Abram to father a great nation which was followed by a promise of providing him land, seed, and blessing. Therefore, this portion of Scripture in Genesis 14 falls in the Dispensation of Promise or Patriarchal Rule.

Genesis 14:1-10 describes a great battle that involved combat between an alliance of four kings and another force of five kings. The kingdom of Sodom was one of the participating nations in the group of five. Abram's nephew, Lot, lived in Sodom and was taken hostage during the battle. The enemy of Sodom also took Lot's goods as well. One of the other hostages escaped and was able to brief Uncle Abram about his nephew's capture. According to Genesis 14:14-16 Abram took the initiative and set out to free his nephew:

> 14) Now when Abram heard that his brother was taken captive, he armed his three hundred and eighteen trained servants who were born in his own house, and went in pursuit as far as Dan. 15) He divided his forces against them by night, and he and his servants attacked them and pursued them as far as Hobah, which is north of Damascas. 16) So he brought back all the goods, and also brought back his brother Lot and his goods, as well as the women and the people.

This is a significant discovery for us. We have barely scratched the surface of the Scriptures and we find the documentation of an armed hostage rescue. Abram led 318 men who were equipped for battle with the intent of killing the hostage takers in order to free those who were held captive. Not only was his plan lethal, it was practical and tactical. It was practical because he understood the world in which he lived and only through the use of violence would he be able to succeed in his mission. His plan was tactical because he divided his forces and attacked at night. The darkness would conceal the size of his forces and make it difficult for the enemy to see his approach.

Through the use of deadly force Abram was able to rescue Lot, the other captives, and reclaim their stolen property. Although the number is not recorded, there is no doubt many men lost their lives during this rescue. In fact, we will soon view a very informative title that was given to this specific battle by the author of the book of Hebrews.

According to Genesis 14:17, Abram defeated all four of the kings in combat during this operation. Abram returned from the battle and was met by the king of Sodom in the Valley of Shaven, also called the King's Valley. However, there was another very significant person who was there to greet Abram in that valley. His name was Melchizedek.

Melchizedek was the king of Salem. Salem was the name of the area that we now know as Jerusalem. Genesis 14:18 tells us he was also the priest of God Most High. Melchizedek is a very important figure in the Bible because of his connection with Christ Himself. Melchizedek is actually called a "type" of Christ. This is a term used in the doctrine of Typology. The "type" is the one who is a foreshadowing of the "anti-type." Therefore, Melchizedek is considered the type while Jesus is the anti-type.

There are several reasons why Melchizedek is considered a type of the Messiah Jesus. He was a King of Jerusalem. He was also a priest of God who served Abram and to whom Abram gave a tithe although Melchizedek was not in the Levite tribe. His name also means "King of Righteousness." The Scriptures provide more explicit connections between Melchizedek and Jesus Christ in Psalm 110, and Hebrews 5 and 7.

As I mentioned before, Melchizedek came out to meet with Abram after he returned from waging successful combat. In fact, the battle is described as "the slaughter of the kings" in Hebrews 7:1. Genesis 14:18-20 provides the details of Melchizedek's greeting to Abram:

> 18) Then Melchizedek King of Salem brought out bread and wine; he was the priest of God Most High. 19) And he blessed him and said: "Blessed be Abram of God Most High, Possessor of heaven and earth; 20) And Blessed be God Most High, Who has delivered your enemies into your hand." And he gave him a tithe of all.

Melchizedek, the priest of God, blessed Abram. In the Biblical context a blessing upon an individual would typically follow a performance of obedience or righteousness. Melchizedek also revealed that God was with Abram and delivered his enemies into Abram's hand.

Melchizedek's blessing must have been so encouraging to Abram. More importantly it was the evidence that Abram's rescue operation, which involved bearing weapons and killing Lot's hostage takers, was declared a justified act by the priest of God Most High and the LORD Himself.

Psalms, hymns, and spiritual songs have been utilized to worship God for thousands of years. These same songs frequently reveal very much about Christ and His character. Turn with me to Exodus 15 where we will study a very interesting song written by the prophet Moses.

Moses

The great prophet Moses and the people of Israel sang a song to the LORD in response to being redeemed from slavery in Egypt.

This song, which is commonly known as the "Song of Moses," is recorded in Exodus 15:1-18. Israel's Hero and Deliverer, the LORD God, had led them out of Egypt where they suffered hard-labor slavery for over 400 years. Israel also witnessed the strength of the LORD when He utterly destroyed the Egyptian army in the Red Sea as revealed in Exodus 14:30-31:

> 30) So the LORD saved Israel that day out of the hand of the Egyptians, and Israel saw the Egyptians dead on the seashore. 31) Thus Israel saw the great work which the LORD had done in Egypt; so the people feared the LORD, and believed the LORD and His servant Moses.

Before we move on I should provide some clarity on the very distinctive relationship Moses enjoyed with the LORD. God shared with Moses' brother and sister, Aaron and Miriam, the details of this relationship in Numbers 12:6-8:

> 6) Then He said, "Hear now My words: If there is a prophet among you, I, the LORD, make Myself known to him in a vision; I speak to him in a dream.7) Not so with My servant Moses; He is faithful in all My house. 8) I speak to him face to face, Even plainly, and not in dark sayings; And he sees the form of the LORD. Why then are you not afraid To speak against My servant Moses?"

The LORD confirmed that His relationship with Moses was unique. For Moses to meet with the LORD "face to face" is an indication the prophet experienced intimate fellowship with the LORD. As a result of this special relationship with the Creator of the universe, Moses provided us with some very interesting information about the LORD Himself in this Song of Moses. Moses wrote in Exodus 15:3:

> 3) The LORD is a man of war; The LORD is His name.

139

The LORD is a man of war? We will later address the issue of war in this claim but Moses just described The LORD as a man. This is not an uncommon occurrence in the Scriptures, especially in the Older Testament. This type of writing is known as an anthropomorphic description of God. "Anthropo" means "man" while "morphe" means "in form of." The anthropomorphic literature in the Bible normally ascribes man-like physical characteristics to God although He is Spirit.

There are other anthropomorphic examples in the same song, such as in verses 6 and 8, where the LORD is said to have hands and nostrils. Since the LORD was solely Spirit when the Hebrew Scriptures were revealed and the incarnation of God the Son had not yet occurred, then to say He is a man of war would be anthropomorphic. Yet, is it actually an anthropomorphic description? My question will make better sense later when we study end-times combat in the book of Revelation.

It is indeed an intriguing concept that the LORD is a man of war. The prophet Moses exposed that the Creator of the universe is a warrior which is incredibly revealing considering the topic of our investigation. We are now better equipped to understand the heart of God and comprehend the LORD's occasional aggressive demeanor when He intervenes in human experience. Since we live in a violent world His intervention shall logically require the use of deadly force at times in order to accomplish His purposes.

Moses was assigned and inspired by the Spirit of Christ to write the above Scripture disclosing this truth of the LORD. As a warrior Himself, He naturally provided guidance to His people through the same prophet in regards to waging war against their enemies. Let's turn now to the book of Deuteronomy and view the rules of combat specifically written for the nation of Israel.

Deuteronomy 20

The LORD's directive to Israel on the issue of waging war is documented in Deuteronomy 20 which is a portion of Scripture that falls in the Dispensation of the Mosaic Law. There are several logical reasons why God would give instruction in the practice of war to His chosen national people. In fact, He provided some specificity while explaining His purpose for bringing the nation of Israel out of Egypt in Leviticus 25:38:

> 38) 'I am the LORD your God, who brought you out of the land of Egypt, to give you the land of Canaan and to be your God.

The land of Canaan consisted of the area promised to Abram and his descendents in Genesis 15:18-21. Since the land was currently occupied by people, Israel would be required to take the land by force. Israel would have a future of waging war so it makes perfect sense God would give some guidance on the topic. It's also interesting how the LORD made a connection between the nation's occupation of the land and the reality of His relationship to Israel as their God. This connection will be more obvious as we continue our study of Deuteronomy 20.

In Deuteronomy 20:1-4 God began by giving directives on keeping the soldiers of Israel motivated and encouraged as they prepared to go out to battle. The priest was assigned the duty to speak to the people who were on the verge of entering the hostile theater. He was to remind them that the LORD, Who delivered them from the mighty Egyptian army, was going to battle with them and for them. In other words, He would save Israel from their enemies.

In Deuteronomy 20:5-9 the officers were assigned to cull out the people who were not willing to fight in order to find those who were prepared for battle. The officers were to ask for those men who had built a house but had not dedicated it, those men who had planted a vineyard but had not yet eaten of it, those men who were betrothed to a woman but had not yet married her, and those men who were fearful and fainthearted. The men who fell into these four categories were exempt from combat.

According to verse 8 there was a concern the fear of those who were fainthearted may become contagious and cause their brethren to become fearful as well. Finally, the officers were to choose men to be captains and lead sections of armies into battle. There is another exemption listed in Deuteronomy 24:5 where a newly married man was free from going to battle for one year so he may bring happiness to his wife.

The next directive in Deuteronomy 20:10 will aid us in understanding some of the actions taken by the nation of Israel in her future. The LORD commanded Israel that when they drew near to a city with the intentions of fighting against it they were to proclaim an "offer of peace." If the city accepted the offer they were to serve Israel. However, if the city refused the offer and chose war instead Israel was to besiege the city.

The LORD provided specific "rules of engagement" in Deuteronomy 20:13-17, particularly on who Israel was to kill during their military assault. The Israelites were to kill every male while battling certain cities. In those same cities they were to spare the women, the children, and the livestock with all its spoil. They also were to eat of the enemies' plunder.

These cities were described in verse 15 as those that are "very far from you, which are not the cities of these nations." These were also the cities who received the "offer of peace" prior to the engagement. On the other hand, the battle instructions to Israel for warring against the "these nations" and the nations themselves are described in Deuteronomy 20:16-18:

> 16) "But of the cities of these peoples which the LORD your God gives you as an inheritance, you shall let nothing that breathes remain alive,17) "but you shall utterly destroy them: the Hittite and the Amorite and the Canaanite and the Perizzite and the Hivite and the Jebusite, just as the LORD your God has commanded you,18) "lest they teach you to do according to all their abominations which they have done for their gods, and you sin against the LORD your God.

The LORD didn't fail to explain His reason for this extreme requirement. These nations inhabited the land God promised to Abram as an inheritance for His people. The LORD waited for over four hundred years until finally exacting judgment on the people of these nations for their extreme sin, or for the "iniquity of the Amorites to be complete" as spoken of in Genesis 15:7-16. The LORD was concerned Israel would be seduced into emulating their abominable worship to false gods which even involved the sacrificing of their children to demons (Psalm106:34-39). Therefore, each of the nations had to be completely destroyed.

As you can imagine, this would require an enormous amount of fortitude by each and every soldier of Israel. Soldiers are trained to kill other soldiers in battle. But to kill every living thing would involve taking the lives of even the women and the little children. It was essential for Israel's military members to place their faith in God in order to complete such a task as well as to mentally process their actions and prevent themselves from being overwhelmed with guilt. Regardless of this brutal reality, by faith they would except it was justified since it was commanded by God Himself. The "offer of peace" described back in verse 10 was not to be given to these nations.

The understanding of the dispensations is exceptionally important in this particular situation. These rules of war are not universal. The LORD gave these directives to Israel and they are exclusively for His national people. He was not revealing universal principles of war to be followed by every country of the world. Israel would inherit or posses these lands which needed eradication of evil. The LORD chose to utilize Israel during the process instead of executing it Himself as He did in Sodom and Gomorrah (Genesis 19:1-29).

An additional and significant point is that the "these nations" were not caught unaware by Israel's aggressive tactics. It is abundantly clear in the Scriptures that these nations had military intelligence on what the LORD was accomplishing through Israel prior to the nation's arrival in the land. There was plenty of warning and time to vacate the land in order to save the lives of their people. A woman in Jericho named Rahab provided the evidence of this knowledge as she explained to the Jewish spies how her people had already known about the LORD and Israel's conquest of the land according to Joshua 2:1-11.

These spies were seeking intelligence on the city of Jericho for a future attack by Israel. This would be the initial battle of the invasion of the land. As I explained earlier, the LORD elected Israel to remove the evil from the land via war. However, we will soon witness there was a closer relationship between the LORD and Israel's military victories particularly while being led by the great warrior and leader, Joshua.

Joshua

We can observe the implementation of Israel's rules of combat in the book of Joshua. Joshua had already demonstrated his trust in the God of Israel when he and Caleb wanted to take the land 40 years prior. As a result, he succeeded Moses as Israel's leader after the great prophet's death. The LORD revealed in Joshua 1:1-4 that the new commander would lead the nation in taking the land promised to his forefathers. God also added an encouraging reminder recorded in Joshua 1:9:

> 9) "Have I not commanded you? Be strong and of good courage; do not be afraid, nor be dismayed, for the LORD your God is with you wherever you go."

Joshua believed the LORD and led Israel through many battles as they were taking over the land of promise. A popular battle during this campaign was the assault on Jericho which is documented in Joshua 6. Joshua however had a very significant and revealing experience just prior to that operation.

In Joshua 5:13-15 we are told Joshua encountered an intriguing Individual. Joshua was by Jericho when he saw a Man opposite him Who had His sword drawn. Israel's commander approached Him and inquired if He was for Israel or for their enemy. The Man introduced Himself as the Commander of the army of the LORD. Joshua's reaction was to fall on his face as a sign of worship and addressed the Man by saying, "What does my Lord say to His servant?"

According to this passage the Commander of the army of the LORD didn't rebuke Joshua for worshiping Him which is typically how an angel would react. The Man told him to remove his sandal for he was standing on a holy place. This should sound familiar for this is what God commanded Moses as He spoke to Moses from the burning bush in Exodus 3:5. There is no doubt this was God temporarily in human form prior to the incarnation of Christ.

This type of experience is often called a Christophany, a pre-incarnate appearance of God the Son. Joshua was speaking to the pre-incarnate Christ who was a foreshadowing of the "Man of War" described in Exodus 15. The true "Man of War" will be disclosed later in this book. The Commander of the army of the LORD was fulfilling the promise from Joshua 1:9 that He would be with Joshua wherever he went.

Israel was victorious in their battle with Jericho only after the LORD brought down the walls of the city. However, Israel's future war campaign was hindered after that battle because of an Israelite named Achan. Achan had violated the command of the LORD found in Joshua 6:18. The order was to abstain from the accursed things in that land. He defied the ordinance by confiscating certain items while in Jericho which cursed all of Israel. Because of that violation, Israel was unable to defeat her next enemy located in the city of Ai.

God revealed to Joshua the trespass that Achan had committed (Joshua 7:11-12). God also told him Israel would continue to be defeated unless the accursed was destroyed. Joshua and Israel later stoned and burned Achan and his family for his violation of the command. Once this was finished, Israel resumed her victorious war campaign through the land of Canaan which is documented in Joshua chapters 8-11.

The battles were definitely brutal as Israel followed the very rules of engagement that were provided to the nation by God in Deuteronomy 20. After Achan was executed, Israel's victorious operation resumed with their assault on the city of Ai. Israel utterly destroyed the city of Ai by killing the entire population of 12,000 inhabitants (Joshua 8:25-26).

Israel fought battle after battle as the conquest of the land continued. The Israeli military demonstrated their faith in the LORD for there were times that all that breathed were destroyed and none were left breathing (Joshua 10:40 and 11:11). Eventually Joshua gave the whole land to Israel as an inheritance and the land rested from war (Joshua 11:23).

The LORD was indeed with Joshua and Israel during this violent and successful campaign through the land of Canaan. Yet, the national obedience that Israel displayed with Joshua would later fade. God would continue to glorify Himself in the context of deadly force during this period of Israel's national disobedience known as the times of the Judges.

The Judges

As we move forward in time we arrive at a point of Israel's existence considered the "time of the Judges." This period is also in the Dispensation of the Mosaic Law. The book of Judges covers over three hundred years of Israel's history between the death of Joshua in the early 14th century B.C. and the beginning of the Hebrew Kings in 1050 B.C.

The Hebrew title of this book is pronounced "Shophetim" which means "judges," "rulers," "deliverers," or "saviors." Shophetim not only carries the idea of maintaining justice and settling disputes, but is also used to connote "liberation" and "deliverance."(43)

This time period of Israel's history was one of moral depravity. The nation was still without a king to judge them which evidently also led to their falling away from the Law of God. Judges 21:25 discloses the specifics of the nation's leadership and moral status:

25) "In those days there was no king in Israel; everyone did what was right in his own eyes."

The cycle that would be repeated over and over during this time period began with God's blessing upon Israel. The nation would eventually fall into sinful worship of idols which would provoke God to judgment consisting of the domination of Israel by another pagan people. Israel would cry out for mercy and God would rescue them through a judge who would lead the nation through a military victory resulting in restoration and blessing.

There are seven such cycles recorded in the book of Judges. As you can imagine, there were many battles fought by Israel during this time period. I have decided to investigate four of the judges and their experiences as national saviors. It will be important to lock the last three into our memory for we'll again see their names, such as Barak and Gideon, later in our investigation. I'll introduce the last judge of our inquiry near the end of this section. However, I want to first look at a somewhat unique situation which involved a deliverer named Ehud found in Judges 3:12-30.

Ehud

It's recorded in Judges 3:12 that Israel again did evil in the sight of the LORD which resulted in God's condemnation. The LORD's nation experienced the consequence of being overcome by a man named Eglon, the king of Moab. Israel served under King Eglon for eighteen years. The nation eventually cried out to the LORD and He provided a deliverer named Ehud who is described as a left-handed man. Israel decided that this judge would personally deliver a tribute to King Eglon.

Ehud made himself a double-edged dagger and carried it on his right thigh under his clothing. He delivered the tribute to the king and then had those who had accompanied him to leave the area. Ehud revealed to Eglon that he had a message for him so the king sent his own people away in order to hear it. This gave Ehud the opportunity to draw closer to his target.

The judge removed his dagger and thrust it into Eglon's belly. According to Judges 3:17, the king was a very fat man. When Ehud shoved the dagger in Eglon it was with such great force that the hilt also penetrated causing the fat to close over the blade. The king's entrails came out after Ehud removed the dagger. The deliverer of Israel was able to escape and the king was later found dead by his people in the upper room (Judges 3:25).

This is the unique situation I spoke of earlier. Ehud, a deliverer from God to Israel, executed a tactical assassination of an enemy king. We can assume this was good in the sight of God by what happened afterward.

Ehud later led the rest of the children of Israel into battle against Moab and killed 10,000 of Moab's "stout men of valor" and not one escaped. Then there was rest in the land for 80 years (Judges 3:27-30). The LORD restored Israel through the brave actions of Ehud who went deep into the enemy's nest to kill the king of the nation that oppressed his people and afterward led Israel into victory on the battle field.

Barak

The Lord raised up a female judge named Deborah who was a prophetess (Judges 4:4). Deborah recruited a man by the name of Barak during the time Israel was suffering judgment from God under the hand of Jabin, king of Canaan. We find in Judges 4:15 that Barak eventually led an army under the guidance of the LORD Himself and destroyed the Canaanite army. The Canaanite commander, Sisera, fled the battle field on foot. Judges 4:17-21 states that Sisera had a tent peg driven through his temple into the ground by a woman named Jael. According to Judges 5:31, King Jabin was later conquered by Israel and the land rested again for 40 years.

Gideon

The intriguing military campaign of Gideon is found in Judges 6-8. Israel was experiencing judgment under the Midianites who would fight against them at times along with the Amalekites and the people of the East. Gideon was visited and recruited by the Angel of the LORD, another pre-incarnate appearance of Christ, to lead the children of Israel against the Midianite army of about 135,000 with only 300 Israelite warriors. The LORD caused the enemy to commit intentional fratricide within their camp as the 300 executed the attacked "without" weapons (Judges 7:8-22).

Gideon pursued two fleeing enemy leaders and their 15,000 troops. The judge captured the leaders, Zebah and Zalmunna, and destroyed the enemy army. Gideon then backtracked and killed the men in the city of Penuel for failing to give the Israeli soldiers food as they pursued the enemy. They also disciplined the elders of the people of Succoth for the same reason. Gideon later killed Zebah and Zalmunna after Gideon's son, Jether, displayed the lack of fortitude to draw the sword and execute the two leaders. According to Judges 8:28, the country then rested for 40 years.

Although Gideon's career as a judge is fairly renowned, there is still the experience of one other deliverer that quite possibly is even more legendary. Most people would recognize the name of this popular Biblical figure because of songs and bedtime stories. However, I am confident that a significant number of those persons don't know that he was one of these judges of Israel. The man I am speaking of is Samson and next we will investigate the Scriptures that document his life.

Samson

The record of Samson actually begins in Judges Chapter 13 which covers the events prior to his birth. Israel was suffering judgment again while under the hand of the Philistines. Samson's father, Manoah, was visited by the Angel of the LORD and was told his barren wife would have a child. The child was to be raised as a Nazarite to God, according to Judges 13:5.

The Nazarite was to be a special man in his discipline and obedience to the LORD while he lived in accordance to the directives found in Numbers 6. An excellent example is John the Baptist, the cousin of the Lord Jesus, who was also called to live by the Nazarite vow (Luke 1:13-15).

The Angel of the LORD also prophesied Manoah's son would be a deliverer for the nation of Israel to bring them out from under the hand of the Philistines. The son, who was called Samson, was born and the LORD blessed him and the Spirit of the LORD began to move upon him (Judges 13:24-25). We will soon witness the significance of this relationship between Samson and the Spirit of the LORD as we continue to examine the life of this great liberator.

Judges 14:4 explains that the LORD was using the women of the enemy to draw Samson to an opportunity to move against the Philistines. While Samson walked through the area of the vineyards of Timnah he was attacked by a lion. Judges 14:6 reveals the following:

> 6) And the **Spirit of the LORD**(emphasis mine) came mightily upon him, and he tore the lion apart as one would have torn apart a young goat, though he had nothing in his hand. But he did not tell his father or his mother what he had done.

Against the will of his parents, Samson married a woman from Timnah, a daughter of the Philistines. Samson later told a riddle to some of the men of his wife's people. After several days of not being able to answer the riddle, the men threatened to burn Samson's wife and her father's house if she did not entice the judge to explain the riddle (Judges 14:15). Samson explained the riddle to his wife and she finally was able to share it with the men. The men eventually attempted to bring a riddle to Samson as well and his reaction is recorded in Judges 14:19:

> 19) Then the **Spirit of the LORD**(emphasis mine) came upon him mightily, and he went down to Ashkelon and killed thirty of their men, took their apparel, and gave the changes of clothing to those who had explained the riddle. So his anger was aroused, and he went back to his father's house.

We find a similar situation involving Samson in Judges 15. The judge was persuaded by his own people to be placed under arrest and given to the Philistines. As a result, Samson was bound by two new ropes and the men of Judah began to escort him to the

Philistines (Judges15:13-14a). According to Judges 14b-15 the following occurred:

> 14b) Then the **Spirit of the LORD** (emphasis mine) came mightily upon him; and the ropes that were on his arms became like flax that is burned with fire, and his bonds broke loose from his hands. 15) He found a fresh jawbone of a donkey, reached out with his hand and took it, and killed a thousand men with it.

It's abundantly clear the Spirit of the LORD consistently empowered Samson in his acts of deadly force resulting in the victorious outcomes of his battles. However, something significant happened after Samson killed the 1,000 men with the jawbone of the donkey. He became very thirsty as a result of his efforts and needed water for restoration. Evidently his thirst was so intense he thought he was going to die and fall into the hands of the enemy (Judges 15:18). God's response is recorded in verse 19:

> 19) So God split the hollow place that is in Lehi, and water came out, and he drank; and his spirit returned, and he revived. Therefore he called its name En Hakkore, which is in Lehi to this day.

Not only did the Spirit of the LORD lead Samson during this victorious battle, but God demonstrated His pleasure with him by splitting the ground and providing the life-restoring water so that he may live and not fall into the hands of the Philistines. He provided life to Samson, not death or captivity. God rewarded Samson after a ferocious engagement with the enemy in which 1,000 men were slain by this judge of Israel.

The story of Samson is one of great popularity particularly due to the relationship that he had with a women named Delilah. This relationship would lead to his demise but not without one final blow to the enemy by the hand of Samson himself. We find the record of how this portion of his life unfolded in Judges 16:16-30.

Delilah eventually pestered Samson enough to cause him to divulge the source of his tremendous strength. His strength came of course from the LORD but there was also a connection with his unshaven head and the LORD's gift of that strength. Samson knew if his head was shaved he would become like any mere man in regards to his power and ability to fight (Judges 16:17). The Philistines were led to Samson while he slept where his seven locks were shaved from his head. Samson finally awoke prepared to fight off the Philistines as he did in previous engagements. However, the judge was not aware of one important detail found in Judges 16:20c:

> 20c) But he did not know that the LORD had departed from him.

Unlike what we have seen in previous passages, the Spirit of the LORD was not available to come mightily upon Samson. The hair ordinance of the Nazirite had been violated which obviously disrupted his fellowship with the LORD. More importantly, Samson could not defend himself from an enemy whom he had already dealt many losses to in the past. The reality of his vulnerability was demonstrated when the Philistines were able to arrest Samson. They put out his eyes, secured him with bronze fetters, and forced him to be a grinder in their prison.

The Philistines rejoiced in response to their victory over this great judge of Israel. They gave credit to their god, Dagon, for delivering Samson into their custody. They prepared a great sacrifice for Dagon and had a grand ceremony in their god's sacrificial temple. Samson was later escorted there to perform for all the guests. The

Scripture indicates there where about 3,000 men and women, consisting of all the lords of the Philistines, attending this celebration on the temple's roof.

After Samson was brought from the prison to the temple, he asked to be placed between the temple's supporting pillars. Israel's judge had a plan and some of his hair evidently had grown back. Samson then initiated his unexpected offensive against the Philistines as described in Judges 16:28:

> 28) Then Samson called to the LORD, saying, "O Lord God, remember me, I pray! Strengthen me, I pray, just this once, O God, that I may with one blow take vengeance on the Philistines for my two eyes!"

Samson then placed his hands on one pillar to his left and one to his right. He braced himself against the pillars and said in verse 30a:

> 30a) "Let me die with the Philistines!"

Samson pushed against the pillars causing the temple to come crashing upon the lords of the Philistines. The result of this heroic act is recorded in verse 30c:

> 30c) So the dead that he killed at his death were more than he had killed in his life.

As a reminder, this occurred after Samson caved and revealed to Delilah the secret of his strength. The LORD left Samson which not only led to his capture, but also gave the wicked enemy reason to showcase their false god as victorious. The LORD showed mercy and grace while He answered Samson's last prayer to defeat the adversary. He granted Samson strength giving him the opportunity to kill more of the enemy than he had killed in all of his lifetime.

It is also interesting that Samson actually sacrificed his own life in his final blow to the Philistines. This was definitely a selfless tactical assassination because Samson gave his life to destroy much of the enemy's leadership.

Perhaps you are wondering if there is more evidence proving the LORD was pleased with the actions of these Judges which involved killing the enemy. We shall soon view another portion of Scripture that confirms God's opinion of these men, specifically Gideon, Barak, and Samson. Before we research that passage of the Bible, I would like for us to investigate the life of Israel's great warrior king, David, and his use of deadly force and killing on the battle field.

King David

David was the second official king of Israel. He succeeded Saul who did not please the LORD with his kingship or his personal obedience to His commands. For example, Saul was instructed by God to attack and punish Amalek for ambushing Israel as the nation came up from Egypt (1 Samuel 15:2-3). The LORD said in verse 3:

> 3) 'Now go and attack Amalek, and utterly destroy all that they have, and do not spare them. But kill both man and woman, infant and nursing child, ox and sheep, and camel and donkey.'"

God obviously took this attack upon His people very serious for nothing was to be left alive in the assault. Saul attacked Amalek and utterly destroyed everyone but one person. He captured the king, Agag, and brought back all of the best in livestock (1 Samuel 15:7-9). This was in violation of what was commanded to him by the LORD. Eventually the prophet Samuel addressed Saul about his disobedience. Samuel had Agag brought to him and the pagan king pleaded for his life. 1 Samuel 15:33 explains the prophet's response:

> 33) But Samuel said, "As your sword has made women childless, so shall your mother be childless among women." And Samuel hacked Agag in pieces before the LORD in Gilgal.

1 Samuel 16 begins with the LORD's process of removing Saul and replacing him with another as king over Israel. He sent Samuel to Jesse the Bethlehemite because the LORD had chosen for Himself a king from among his sons (1 Samuel 16:1). He expressed to Samuel that He made his choice based upon the heart of the son rather than outward appearance (1 Samuel 16:7). Seven sons of Jesse were displayed before Samuel, yet there was still the youngest son who was out tending the sheep. The young shepherd David was eventually presented before the LORD and He announced the following in 1 Samuel 16:12c:

> 12c) And the LORD said, "Arise, anoint him; for he is the one!"

David was anointed by Samuel and according to 1 Samuel 16:13, the Spirit of the LORD came upon the young shepherd from that day forward. The Scripture again exposes the ministry of God's Spirit, the Spirit of Christ, in the lives of these warriors. David later became King Saul's armor bearer and they developed a loving relationship.

1 Samuel 17 presents the popular showdown between Goliath of the Philistines and young David. Goliath had taunted the men of Israel and raised great fear in their hearts. David approached King Saul and made his request to fight Goliath himself. Although it was offered to

him, David refused to wear the King's armor and went out to battle the giant with only a staff, a sling, and five stones (1 Samuel 17:40).

In 1 Samuel 17:49-51 we are able to review David's actions and his went out to fight the great warrior hero of the Philistines. He used his sling and struck Goliath with a stone to the forehead. David's delivery was with deadly accuracy causing the giant to fall face first to the ground. The young warrior followed up by drawing Goliath's own sword and cutting off his head with it. The response of the rest of Goliath's army is recorded in 1 Samuel 17 verse 51b:

> 51b) And when the Philistines saw that their champion was dead, they fled.

David's victory motivated the hearts of his people. The warriors of Israel and Judah responded to the young shepherd's kill by rising up with a shout and pursuing the Philistine army. After returning from the chase they seized the property from the tents of the enemy. David carried the head of Goliath back to Jerusalem for all to witness and celebrate his defeat of Israel's enormous adversary (1 Samuel 17:52-54).

This was the beginning of David's great military career although he was not yet officially king of Israel. Unfortunately it was also the beginning of the end to the relationship between Saul and David. According to 1 Samuel 18:6-7, women from many of the cities of Israel arrived to meet King Saul and David as they returned from the slaughter of the Philistine. The tension between David and Saul was inflamed by the words sung by the women in verse 7:

> 7) So the women sang as they danced, and said: "Saul has slain his thousands, And David his ten thousands."

Saul became angry and displeased with David. Saul eyed David from that day forward. The king was jealous of David and saw that the kingdom was well within David's grasp because of the famous military victory. Saul also was afraid of David for he knew that the LORD had departed from him and now was with David (1 Samuel 18:12, 14-15). From this time until the death of Saul, David was threatened, pursued, and attacked by the king.

My intention for investigating the life of David is not to cover every battle he fought or how many enemies he killed. I want to demonstrate how David, who was also a prophet of God (Matthew 22:41-45, Acts 2:29-35), considered his ability to lead as Israel's warrior king to be a gift from the LORD Himself. For instance, David is quoted as saying in Psalm 18:31-34:

> 31) For who is God, except the LORD? And who is a rock, except our God? 32) It is God who arms me with strength, and makes my way perfect. 33) He makes my feet like the feet of deer, And sets me on my high places. 34) He teaches my hands to make war, So that my arms can bend a bow of bronze.

The prophet David again praised God for his capacity to fight in Psalm 144:1-2:

> 1) A Psalm of David. Blessed be the LORD my Rock, Who trains my hands for war, And my fingers for battle- 2) My lovingkindness and my fortress, My high tower and my deliverer, My shield and the One in whom I take refuge, Who subdues my people under me.

David gave God the credit and the glory for providing him the skill to fight in battles for his country. However, he also mentioned a more domestic issue. The LORD empowered him to police his own people with the same hands and fingers that are trained for war and battle.

Evidently he was also responsible as the king for taking care of civil unrest. It was the military's additional duty to act as peace officers which required arresting violators of the law to maintain civil order. Israel's king advised how one should approach the violator during an arrest situation in 2 Samuel 23:2-7:

> 2) "The Spirit of the LORD spoke by me, and His word was on my tongue. 3) The God of Israel said, The Rock of Israel spoke to me: 'He who rules over men must be just, ruling in the fear of God. 4) And he shall be like the light of the morning when the sun rises, A morning without clouds, Like the tender grass springing out of the earth, By clear shining after rain.' 5) "Although my house is not so with God, Yet He has made with me an everlasting covenant, Ordered in all things and secure. For this is all my salvation and all my desire; Will He not make it increase? **6) But the sons of rebellion shall all be as thorns thrust away, Because they cannot be taken with hands. 7) But the man who touches them Must be armed with Iron and the shaft of the spear, And they shall be utterly burned with fire in their place.**"(emphasis mine)

David warned the one who will "take" one of these "sons of rebellion" should be ready for battle. There is no indication David was speaking of national or war combat in this passage. It appears David was actually addressing domestic issues. This is the responsibility of "he who rules over men" in verse 3. The king and those in the government under him provide security in the land by exacting justice over those whom he ruled. In addition, this passage seems to convey a universal principle for all kings of the earth to heed rather than an exclusive principle for Israel alone.

The process of serving justice often requires the seizure of those who violate the law or rebel against the government. David admonished us to be armed for battle when we go to affect that seizure or arrest. If the prophet and warrior king David said to be armed, it is for a purpose. The arresting authority should be prepared to use deadly force if that wanted person should resist in a manner that warrants such action. Of course, deadly force should be used in the domestic realm according to the rules of law adopted by each nation, state, or civilization.

The Scriptures clearly teach that David was involved in a large amount of killing and bloodshed in his life time. Because of his career on the battlefield the LORD would later deny David a special request. Yet he was not considered a murderer as a result of his combat experience. On the contrary, David was a true warrior in the sense he showed amazing self-control and restraint. For instance, there was an interesting incident which occurred while David and his men were on the run from King Saul.

According to 1 Samuel 24:1-11, Saul took three thousand men and stalked David and his men in the Rocks of the Wild Goats. They had hidden themselves from Saul in the recesses of a certain cave in that area. King Saul's path led him to the very same cave where he entered to take care of his needs. David's men reminded him that the LORD said He would deliver David's enemy into his hands to do with him as he saw fit.

David was eventually able to get close enough to Saul to cut off a corner of the king's robe. However, notice David's intriguing response to his servants in 1 Samuel 24 verse 6:

> 6) And he said to his men, "The LORD forbid that I should do this thing to my master, The LORD's anointed, to stretch out my hand against him, seeing he is the anointed of the LORD."

David had the chance to kill the one who wrongfully pursued him. Instead, his love for the LORD and for His anointed, King Saul, led him to show great restraint and self-control. He later revealed the mercy he had demonstrated by showing Saul the corner of his robe that David had removed while the king was in the cave.

This proved David had no ill-gotten motives for taking the kingdom by force. David's heart was troubled even by the fact he had cut Saul's robe (1 Samuel 24:5). After considering David's words and actions during this incident, does it appear that he had a heart of a murderer? I think not!

David also demonstrated his self-control during an account we visited earlier involving a very fortunate man named Shimei. This incident in which David showed great restraint and wisdom is found in 2 Samuel 16:5-13. He was now king of Israel and traveled into the area known as Bahurim. Shimei, who was one of the men from the house of Saul, came out to let David have a piece of his mind.

According to verse 6 Shimei threw stones at David and his mighty men. This was a very dangerous act for David's 37 mighty men were nothing less than "bad to the bone" in regards to warfare and killing. They also were tremendously loyal to King David.

2 Samuel 23: 8-39 identifies these mighty men and provides some details of their great victories in battle. For example, a man named Abishai is listed as one of David's mighty men in that passage. Abishai is said to have killed 300 men with his spear and became one of the three captains of the 37 mighty men.

Evidently Shimei did not consider the possible deadly consequences for he also called David out by yelling, "Come out! Come out! You bloodthirsty man, you rogue!" Unfortunately for Shimei, there was another person who heard his disrespectful rant to the anointed king of Israel. According to 2 Samuel 16:9 one of the mighty men, Abishai, was present and responded by saying to David:

> 9) "Why should this dead dog curse my Lord the King? Please, let me go over and take off his head!"

There is no doubt Abishai meant every word and had the fortitude to take Shimei's head. The great warrior King David responded by refusing Abishai's request (2 Samuel 16:10-12). David even hoped the LORD would see his restraint and bless David thus demonstrating that his security and identity were grounded in his relationship with God.

David was not a stone-cold killer of men. He was a true, self-controlled warrior who knew killing in battle was necessary. He may have even experienced a type of anticipation or longing for the next battle to win, which only warriors would understand. Nonetheless, he was not a bloodthirsty man like Shimei accused him of being. This is just as true even after considering the large number of people who died under the hands of David and his mighty men. Let us now address David's special request that I mentioned earlier that was denied by the LORD.

King David and the Temple

A common concern in regards to the moral status of David's killing is the Lord's response to David's request to build the first temple. God specifically mentioned David's shedding of much blood in battle as the reason why he was denied. Does this mean God considered the king's warrior career as one of sin? We will now investigate this issue because it is such a crucial topic in regards to ascertaining God's true and consistent perspective on the use of deadly force.

In 2 Samuel 7:1-2 David realized he was living in a house of cedar while the ark of God dwelt inside a tent. David was concerned that the ark, where the presence of God dwelt among the Israelites, was not afforded a stable place to stay. Even the LORD conveyed the same predicament in 2 Samuel 7:6:

> 6) "For I have not dwelt in a house since the time that I brought the children of Israel up from Egypt, even to this day, but have moved about in a tent and in a tabernacle.

The tabernacle was a mobile temple. It was transient in nature since the children of Israel were transient themselves moving from place to place especially during the time of Moses. We find in Scripture that David's concern was actually not shared by the LORD. The LORD explained in 2 Samuel 7:7 that He had never asked anyone whom He had chosen to rule over His people, "Why have you not built Me a house of cedar?"

As we continue to study this chapter we shall witness the common problem of man constructing his own ideas and schemes while disregarding the fact that God's plan may contradict them. The next few verses are significant in understanding the LORD's decree for David's life and why the king was denied his desire to build a house for the LORD. Notice God's message in 2 Samuel 7:8-9 which Nathan delivered to David:

> 8) "Now therefore, thus shall you say to my servant David, 'Thus says the LORD of hosts: "I took you from the sheepfold, from following the sheep, to be ruler over my people, over Israel. 9) "And I have been with you wherever you have gone, and have cut off all your enemies

from before you, and have made you a great name, like the name of the great men who are on the earth.

The LORD explained His plan for David's life was to function as the king and to rule over His people. God's desire for King David was to go out, while the LORD was with him, and defeat the enemies of Israel in order to develop a great name for David. The LORD continued explaining His plan for Israel in 2 Samuel 7:10. They were to move around and be in transient. However, He will plant them. They would eventually find a place of stability and need to move no more. Israel had not experienced such a thing yet. But God had a plan for that to soon become a reality and then He would be ready to receive a fixed house for Himself.

The establishment of the Davidic Covenant is recorded in 2 Samuel 7:11-16. The LORD laid out His plan for David and his son. He intended for Israel's rest from their enemies to come as a result of David's warrior ministry. The son of David would succeed him as king and the kingdom would be established forever.

The key verse in this passage for our investigation of the temple is verse 13. The LORD declared the function of building His house of rest would be assigned to David's son, Solomon. David explained to Solomon exactly what the LORD said to him in 1 Chronicles 22: 7-10:

> 7) And David said to Solomon: "My son, As for me, it was in my mind to build a house to the name of the LORD my God; 8) "but the word of the LORD came to me, saying, 'You have shed much blood and have made great wars; you shall not build a house for My name, because you have shed much blood on the earth in my sight. 9) 'Behold, a son shall be born to you, who shall be a man of rest ; and I will give him rest from all of his enemies all

around. His name shall be Solomon, for I will give peace and quietness to Israel in his days.10) 'He shall build a house for My name, and he shall be My son, and I will be his Father; and I will establish the throne of his kingdom over Israel forever.' (See also 1 Chronicles 28:2-7)

There are a few pertinent observations from this passage. Notice the resemblance between Solomon's name in the Hebrew language, (Heb. *Shelomoh*), and the Hebrew word used in the same verse which translates "peace", (Heb. *shalom*). God chose this name for David's son based upon His intended function for Solomon's life as king over Israel.

This revelation was also received by David prior to his adultery with Bethsheba and the murder of her husband, Uriah the Hittite. That sin was not mentioned by the LORD in the context of building the temple. An interesting additional note is that neither of those sins would have occurred if David was out in battle with his men as kings typically did instead of lounging around in Jerusalem (2 Samuel 11:1). But we must let the Scripture speak without distortion. According to the Scripture God mentioned that David's identity as a man of war and of bloodshed was a reason for denying him of his request to build a house for the LORD.

Although this is true, the LORD did not explicitly say David's life as a warrior was sinful. On the contrary, the LORD said He was with David during those years of battling the enemies of Israel (2 Samuel 7:8-9). This indicates that the fighting in which David was involved was condoned and supervised by the LORD. Allow me to illustrate two incidents where God dispatched David into missions that inevitably involved killing.

In 1 Samuel 23:1-5 David received word that the Philistines were fighting against the people of Keilah and were "robbing the threshing floors." David inquired of the Lord if he should go and attack the Philistines. His answer is found in verse 2b:

> 2b) And the LORD said to David, "Go and attack the Philistines, and save Keilah."

David's men were already afraid while they were in Judah. They realized it would be even more dangerous to travel to Keilah in order to fight the Philistines. So David inquired of the LORD a second time in verse 4:

> 4) Then David inquired of the LORD once again. And the LORD answered him and said, "Arise, go down to Keilah. For I will deliver the Philistines into your hand."

David adhered to the LORD's command and by faith in His promise went to Keilah and fought the Philistines. According to verse 5 David "struck them with a mighty blow, and took away their livestock." David led his men to battle and used deadly force in order to save the people of Keilah.

The second example is recorded in 1 Samuel 30:1-19. David and his men arrived into the area called Ziglag and learned that the Amalekites had raided the area and burned the city. Nobody was killed in the raid but they did kidnap their wives, sons, and daughters. David's two wives, Ahinoam and Abigail, were among those who were taken captive. His men were so distraught that they spoke of stoning David. However, David strengthened himself in the LORD and asked Him for guidance in verse 8:

> 8) So David inquired of the LORD, saying, "Shall I pursue this troop? Shall I overtake them?" And He answered him, "Pursue, for you shall surely overtake them and without fail recover all."

The LORD directed David to go and execute a hostage rescue. He took 400 of his men and pursued the hostage takers. He found an informant along the way who eventually led David to the captors' location. David and his men arrived to find the Amalekites celebrating over the great spoil they had taken from the Philistines and Judah. The tactics and outcome of this rescue operation is recorded in 1 Samuel 30:17-19:

> 17) Then David attacked them from twilight until the evening of the next day. Not a man of them escaped, except four hundred young men who rode on camels and fled.18) So David recovered all that the Amalekites had carried away, and David rescued his two wives.19) And nothing of theirs was lacking, either small of great, sons or daughters, spoil or anything which they had taken from them; David recovered all.

There are two common themes in these passages we just investigated. First, David executed two rescue missions. Each of these missions involved killing the raiders and hostage-takers in order to save his people.

Second, David was given the command by God Himself to embark on each of these missions. With this in mind, would it be reasonable or logical to conclude that the LORD considered the killing David committed in battle as sinful? I don't think so.

As you can see, there is nothing restful about being in war. War consists of instability and insecurity. The function that God ordained to David was to be the warrior king who would lead Israel as they experienced unrest while they regularly fought their persistent enemies. This was not a suitable time for a "house of rest" unto the LORD to be built.

Let us now return to 1 Chronicles 7-10. The LORD made a distinction between David's and Solomon's assigned functions in verse 9. Solomon will be a man of rest. Opposite of the life of his father, Solomon would experience rest as God gave Israel days of quietness and peace during the era of his rule.

The enemies of Israel would no longer be a threat and the nation could be still and planted. Therefore, Solomon was chosen to build God's house which symbolized stability to the nation of Israel. Israel would no longer need a transient tabernacle as a place to keep the ark of the LORD for the presence of God would be fixed in Jerusalem.

Although David was not allowed to build the house of the LORD, he was not completely barred from the project. He was given the privilege to make the plans and preparations for the building of the temple and its courts. Scripture reveals that David later gave Solomon these plans which the king made while under the direction of God's Spirit (1 Chronicles 28:11-13). David did not sob over the rejection of actually building the LORD's house. He joined in and used this time to encourage his son who was taking on a great responsibility of building the temple which is not for man, but for the LORD God (1 Chronicles 28:10; 29:1).

There is no Scripture explicitly labeling David's killing and bloodshed in battle as sin. Although the LORD was clearly with David during his lethal campaigns, I still would like to provide the Scripture that specifically identifies David's career in battle as righteous. Let's look at Hebrews 11, which is found in the Newer Testament. It also is found in the Dispensation of Grace.

Hebrews 11 is well known for containing what has been dubbed the "Hall of Faith." The writer of this epistle listed several persons found in the Biblical historical narrative who are known for great demonstrations of faith. These people lived their lives by taking

God at His Word. We can declare with confidence that actions considered to be sinful are not accomplished in faith. It would be just as impossible for someone to perform a deed by faith and label it as sin. Hebrews 11:1-2 and 6 present an explanation of faith:

> 1) Now faith is the substance of things hoped for, the evidence of things not seen. 2) For by it the elders obtained a good testimony.

> 6) But without faith it is impossible to please Him, for he who comes to God must believe that He is, and that He is a rewarder of those who diligently seek Him.

The people listed in Hebrews 11 are considered by God as those who lived their lives according to the above verses. Living by faith is how one pleases God and how one obtains a good testimony or witness of their lives. Faithful actions are not categorized as sin. The specific deeds accomplished by these faithful people were listed so we can observe that which pleased God.

The list of people showcased in this chapter begins with Abel in verse 4. More persons like Enoch, Noah, Abraham, Sarah, Isaac, Jacob, Joseph, and Moses are mentioned too. Even Rahab, the harlot from Jericho, made the list in verse 31. In verses 32-34 we read God's perspective on actions committed by a few warriors we have already studied:

> 32) And what more shall I say? For the time would fail me to tell of Gideon and Barak and Samson and Jephthah, also of David and Samuel and the prophets: 33) who through faith subdued kingdoms, worked righteousness, obtained promises, stopped the mouths of lions, 34) quenched the violence of fire, escaped the edge of the sword, out of weakness were made strong, became valiant in battle, turned to flight the armies of the aliens.

Take note of the actions listed in verses 33-34. They were executed in faith by those described above bringing pleasure to God. All of these actions, including being valiant in battle, were considered acts of faith rather than disobedience or sin. Verse 39 teaches that a good testimony or witness was obtained by these people through faith.

It isn't essential for my personal interpretation of Hebrews 11 to be documented here. The text plainly teaches God's perspective of David's killing and bloodshed in battle. It's also fascinating that the three brave judges of Israel whom we investigated earlier were included by the author of Hebrews 11.

We have gathered from the Scripture that the LORD associated His house of rest with the national security status of the kingdom of Israel. David's reputation as a warrior may have been deemed by God as "inappropriate" for the one who would build His temple, but the Scriptures convey a clear message that David's killing in battle was not considered by God as sinful. On the contrary, the warrior king's valiant actions in combat earned him the honor to be listed with Gideon, Barak, and Samson in the "Hall of Faith."

Solomon was selected to build the temple of God. He experienced peace during his reign over the kingdom. Does that mean that this wise king disagreed with the use of deadly force in contexts such as war and policing? Let's turn to the next section and discover Solomon's perspective on that topic.

Solomon

Solomon is considered in the Scriptures to be the wisest man to ever live in the history of men. It would be negligent to sidestep any guidance he may offer on the topic of Christ's view on deadly force. The process by which Solomon acquired such a distinguished reputation is even more important. According to 1 Kings 3:11-12 the gift of his deep wisdom was given to him by God Himself as a response to Solomon's prayer in verse 9:

> 9) "Therefore give to Your servant an understanding heart to judge Your people, that I may discern between good and evil. For who is able to judge this great people of Yours?"

The LORD heard Solomon's prayer and was pleased with him for not asking for a long life, riches, or victory over his enemies. Then the LORD said in verse 12:

> 12) "behold, I have done according to your words; see, I have given you a wise and understanding heart, so that there has not been anyone like you before you, nor shall any like you arise after you.

The crucial point is that Solomon was and still is considered to be the wisest man to have walked the earth. This wisdom consisted of the ability to discern what is good from what is evil. King Solomon shared this wisdom in the form of Scripture. Therefore it would be beneficial for us to search his writings for any instruction on the issue of deadly force and killing. With that in mind we will begin our search in the book of Ecclesiastes.

The portion of Scripture we will visit is Ecclesiastes 3:1-8 which is located in the Dispensation of the Mosaic Law. In this chapter Solomon encourages us to live life to the fullest and to enjoy the good experiences. The negative events of life shall come and we should not waste our time worrying about the future. The good and hard times are not results of chance or luck. They are in the deliberate design of our Creator which is an extremely significant concept in regards to studying the first eight verses. Solomon provided wisdom in verses 1-8 that help us see the heart of God in regards to killing and war:

> 1) To everything there is a season, A time for every purpose under heaven: 2) A time to be born, And a time to die; A time to plant, and a time to pluck what is planted; 3) A time to **kill**(emphasis mine), and a time to heal; A time to break down, And a time to build up; 4) A time to weep, And a time to laugh; A time to mourn, And a time to dance; 5) A time to cast away stones, And a time to gather stones; A time to embrace, And a time to refrain from embracing; 6) A time to gain, And a time to lose; A time to keep, And a time to throw away; 7) A time to tear, And a time to sew; A time to keep silence, And a time to speak; 8) A time to love, And a time to hate; A time of **war**(emphasis mine), and a time of peace.

Before we address the specifics on killing in this passage, notice what Solomon initially established in the first verse. He declared there are seasons and times for every purpose under heaven. These things mentioned are divinely purposed by God Himself, which understandably can be difficult to fathom.

The tension created from considering this concept is obviously based upon the difficulty of reconciling the relationship between the sovereignty of God and the responsibility of man. The specific topics of killing and war are mentioned in this list of purposes in verses 3 and 8. In addition, they are surrounded by other purposes that would not typically be the topic of debate on whether they are moral or immoral.

There are two other major contextual observations in this portion of Scripture in reference to these cycles of purposes. The LORD led

Solomon to write that there is a time for each of these actions. This would imply the moral status of each of these deeds when accomplished at the "appropriate" time. Solomon explained there is even a time to "hate." The LORD Himself was said to have hated Esau. He also hates "workers of iniquity" and abhors the "bloodthirsty and deceitful man" (Psalm 5:5-6). Malachi the prophet wrote that God hates divorce (Malachi 2:16), and Proverbs 6:16-19 lists seven things the LORD hates as well. These would be examples of morally hating or "times to hate."

With this principle established, there are certain situations when killing and waging war are moral since there is a "time" for each of them as well. We have already determined the administration of capital punishment is indeed righteous, according to the Scriptures. The nation which wages war in defense of its national security or the national security of its allies, even if it involves a preemptive strike, may be considered moral. On the other hand, criminal homicide and unprovoked national violent aggression on another non-threatening country could be considered immoral killing and immoral waging of war.

Solomon's father, King David, experienced his share of attacks upon himself that were unwarranted. He commented on the injustice of assaulting even an enemy without cause in Psalm 7:3-5:

> 3) O LORD my God, if I have done this: If there is iniquity in my hands, 4) If I have repaid evil to him who was at peace with me, Or have plundered my enemy without cause, 5) Let the enemy pursue me and overtake me; Yes, let him trample my life to the earth, And lay my honor in the dust. Selah

Solomon was teaching there are circumstances when killing and war are necessary because of the fallen nature of men and the violent disposition of the life experience in which we temporally dwell. An additional interesting note is the word "kill" in verse 3 is translated from the Hebrew term *"harag"* rather than *"ratsach"* which is the Hebrew term found in Exodus 20:13. Solomon was teaching there is a time to *"harag."*

The second contextual observation is these purposes are universal in nature. In other words, Solomon didn't provide a list of purposes that were limited to the time of his rule or lifetime. They are still in effect today and will continue until the end of the temporal age. They are not bound to a specific era or culture. The concept of Solomon's instruction in Ecclesiastes 3:1-8 is just as true today as it was before his lifetime and shall be in the future.

John the Baptist

Luke 3:1-22 covers the beginning of the ministry of John the Baptist and is located in the Dispensation of the Mosaic Law. Prior to the time of this prophet, Israel had suffered 400 years of silence from God. The LORD had not spoken to His people through the prophets because of their disobedience. John was assigned the duty of calling the nation of Israel to repentance in order to prepare them to accept their coming Messiah. Speaking of the Messiah, Jesus revealed the following to the multitudes about John in Matthew 11:9-11:

> 9) "But what did you go out to see? A prophet? Yes, I say to you, and more than a prophet. 10) For this is he of whom it is written: 'Behold, I send My messenger before Your face, Who will prepare Your way before you.' 11) "Assuredly, I say to you, among those born of women there has not risen one greater than John the Baptist;

The Lord Jesus Himself boasted to the people about John the Baptist. John's ministry was so important that the Savior labeled him as more than a prophet and the greatest born of women. If the Lord has such a high regard for the Baptist, we can assume John's perspective on any specific issue will certainly be a godly one.

According to Luke 3:3, John's ministry to prepare Israel for Jesus consisted of a baptism of repentance for the remission of sins. The term "repentance" carries the meaning of a "change of mind" or a "change of heart." The covenant-related people of God were being called to change their heart about their sin and to return back to fellowship with the LORD. This was to prepare them for the Messiah's arrival. Those who repented indentified themselves with John's ministry by being baptized.

Many people flocked to John in order to discover what was going on and to be baptized. In fact, there were three different groups that asked John for guidance on what they should do. First, the people asked in Luke 3:10, "What shall we do then?" After John gave them guidance he was approached by the tax collectors in verse 12. Luke 3:14 reveals those who sought John's instruction next was a group of soldiers. Notice John's response to them:

> 14) Likewise the soldiers asked him saying, "And what shall we do?" So he said to them, "Do not intimidate anyone or accuse falsely, and be content with your wages."

These soldiers obviously had the primary duty of fighting the enemies of Israel in order to protect their people and the sovereignty of their nation. John would have understood that these warriors kill the enemy to accomplish their objectives. It appears these contemporary soldiers carried an additional duty as well.

Since there was no distinguished group with exclusive domestic policing duties, the military forces must have assumed that task. Evidently they were abusing their powers as peace officers through intimidation and false accusations. These were probably the main tactics for extorting money from the people, whom they were tasked to serve, in order to supplement the soldiers' income.

John was given the opportunity to address these soldiers on the topic of repentance. He chose to direct their attention to the corruption within the ranks. John admonished these military servicemen to be content with their pay so they were not tempted to extort the citizens for more money. However, that which is not present in John's orders is just as interesting.

Again John was approached by these trained killers asking for guidance on what they should do to fulfill the call to repent. John was given the chance to take issue with the way the soldiers were carrying out their lives. If killing on the battlefield or in the arena of domestic policing were sinful, this would have been the place for this godly man to set them straight. Yet John confirmed the righteousness of their duties by affirming their right to be paid for their service. He was aware these soldiers received financial support for serving in the military and standing guard for their nation.

Even the Apostle Paul confirmed the principle that a soldier should go to war while being supported materially and financially by those whom he is serving (Corinthians 9:7 and Romans 13:6). John did not condemn these warriors for their choice of occupation which would potentially involve the killing of other persons in the execution of their duty. This was a great opportunity for these public servants to be warned they were sinning against the LORD simply through their profession as soldiers.

The absence of such a warning indicates the duty of the soldier is righteous in the eyes of this godly man, John the Baptist. Therefore, Christ's perspective of Israel's military service members was that they were fulfilling a just and honorable function for their people. However, one may inquire if God only views the soldiers of Israel as being justified in their work. After all, they are "His" people. We may be able to resolve some of this concern after investigating an actual encounter Jesus had with a certain Roman centurion.

Jesus

Before we start our investigation of the passages that reveal this encounter I again want to set the historical context. During Jesus' lifetime on earth Israel was being occupied by the Roman Empire. Caesar's soldiers and command staff had entered the holy land, which was won in battle, and began to govern the country. Israel was allowed to have her own king but he was not granted complete sovereignty to rule his own nation.

In Matthew 8:1-13 and Luke 7:1-10 a Roman centurion had heard about the Lord Jesus. This commander of men had a servant who became very sick and was on the verge of dying. The servant evidently meant very much to him for he sent a group of Jewish elders to plea with Jesus to come and heal him. The elders told Jesus the centurion was a man who loved their nation and had built them a synagogue. In response to the summons Jesus left with the elders to go to the centurion's house. However, this grateful soldier of Rome sent friends to catch the Savior before he could reach the house in order to deliver the following message recorded in Luke 7:6c-8:

6c) "Lord, do not trouble Yourself, for I am not worthy that You should enter under my roof. 7) "Therefore I did not even think myself worthy to come to You. But say the word, and my servant will be healed. 8) "For I also am a man placed under authority, having soldiers under me. And I say to one, 'Go,' and he goes; and to another, 'Come,' and he comes; and to my servant, 'Do this,' and he does it."

Jesus' fascinating response is revealed in Luke 7:9. He "marveled" at the centurion, turned around, and said to the crowd that was following Him, "I say to you, I have not found such great faith, not even in Israel!" According to verse 10, the centurion's friends returned and found the servant had been healed.

In summary, Jesus received a request from a humble commanding soldier of the empire that was occupying His homeland. The Savior healed the centurion's servant from afar and boasted on his great faith. Similar to John the Baptist's situation earlier, Jesus also had the option to address this faithful disciple's profession if it were indeed evil. Jesus instead fulfilled the centurion's request without sending the commander a message such as, "Go, and sin no more." The Lord certainly would have urged the centurion to leave his profession as a soldier if it were evil or immoral especially since he had just demonstrated his trust in Christ.

With this in mind we can assume Jesus did not rebuke this faithful believer for being a Roman military leader because the centurion's occupation was found to be just and good. Via his position as a military service member, this soldier provided security and safety to the people of his home country as well as to the people of Israel at this time in history. It appears that the Lord generally considers the duties executed by the armed forces of "all nations" as a noble service to the citizens whom they are assigned to protect.

In Luke 14:26-35 Jesus was in the process of admonishing those people who were contemplating on following Him as a disciple. Jesus has high expectations, made evident by His desire for each individual disciple to endure and finish well without abandoning the good work. He began by using the example of one who has planned to build a tower. It is only prudent for that person to first sit down and count the cost of starting and finishing the project. The one who leaves the tower incomplete will be mocked by those who see the unfinished work. Jesus followed up by using another example to emphasize this crucial point in Luke 14:31-32:

> 31) "Or what king, going to make war against another king, does not sit down first and consider whether he is able with ten thousand to meet him who comes against him with twenty thousand? 32) "Or else, while the other is still a great way off, he sends a delegation and asks conditions of peace.

It is important to remember that Jesus was stressing careful consideration prior to choosing the demanding but highly righteous endeavor of following Him as a disciple. The theme of discipleship is what makes this passage so interesting. As a teaching aid, Jesus presented the life experience of a wise king who considers first if he has the means to defeat a rival king prior to committing to war.

The obvious question is: Would Jesus use an example of persons contemplating the commission of evil acts to teach the importance of counting the cost of being His disciple? It appears both of the examples Jesus utilized, building towers and warring kings, are considered by the Lord as noble acts. Perhaps Jesus was alluding to Solomon's wisdom articulated in Proverbs 20:18:

18) Plans are established by counsel; By wise counsel wage war.

It would be prudent and beneficial for us to investigate the Scripture which covers the arrest of Jesus in the garden of Gethsemane. I am anticipating a very legitimate question that may develop after one reads the documentation of this event. The concern may be in reference to Jesus' response to Peter after he drew his sword and cut off the right ear of Malchus, the servant of the high priest.

All four Gospels cover this event although different amounts of information are recorded in each. The passages of Scripture that describe the details of Jesus' arrest are Matthew 26:47-56, Mark 14:43-50, Luke 22:47-53, and John 18:1-12. The section written by John Mark has no recording of what Jesus said to Peter after he struck the servant. Therefore, we shall focus our attention to the other three writings and study the Savior's response. Matthew 26:52-54 reads:

> 52) But Jesus said to him, "Put your sword in its place, for all who take the sword will perish by the sword. 53) "Or do you think that I cannot now pray to my Father, and He will provide Me with more than twelve legions of angels? 54) "How then could the Scriptures be fulfilled, that it must happen thus?"

Luke 22:51 reads:

> 51) But Jesus answered and said, "Permit even this." And He touched his ear and healed him.

John 18:11 reads:

11) So Jesus said to Peter, "Put your sword into the sheath. Shall I not drink the cup which My Father has given Me?"

After examining these three passages we can see one similar idea. Jesus had a mission and Peter's actions were preventing the accomplishment of that mission. The Lord knew He had to be arrested in order to fulfill all of the Hebrew Scriptures that prophesied His atoning death and resurrection. Jesus rebuked Peter only because he was coming close to thwarting the plan of God in regards to the salvation of man.

Peter, a fisherman, actually was demonstrating bravery while taking up arms against trained soldiers to protect his Lord. The dilemma was that Jesus didn't want the protection or He would have summoned legions of angels to annihilate His enemies (Matthew 26:53). This arrest was according to the Father's plan and it was the cup Jesus must drink in order for man to experience eternal life with Him.

Jesus obviously stated truth in Matthew 26:52. If you take up arms with the sword, death by the sword is even more a possibility. The Savior not only wanted the Scriptures to be fulfilled in regards to His death and resurrection, He also didn't want Peter to suffer physical death there in the garden. He had plans for Peter, and the fisherman would have eventually lost the battle against the trained soldiers. Christ had already demonstrated His concern for the physical safety of His disciples when the arrest party arrived seeking Him in John 18:8-9:

8) Jesus answered, "I have told you that I am He. Therefore, if you seek Me, let these go their way." 9) That the saying might be fulfilled which He spoke, "Of those whom You gave Me I have lost none."

The Scripture is clear that Jesus didn't want the disciples to lose their lives during this event. He wanted His arrest to go without further incident that would place His followers in danger. There was still so much for them to accomplish later as leaders of His church.

There is another interesting observation in Jesus' response. The Lord told Peter to place the sword back into the sheath. Jesus did not rebuke Peter for having the weapon and He didn't order Peter to discard it. He had commanded the disciples to carry swords for their own protection, yet they were not told to protect their own King.

During a later conversation between Jesus and Pontius Pilate recorded in John 18:33-36, the Lord gave the Roman governor an explanation of why Peter and the other disciples were not to fight. Pilate had asked Jesus if He was the King of the Jews because it had been the Jews who had delivered Him up to be put to death. Jesus gave the governor the following explanation in John 18:36:

> 36) Jesus answered, "My kingdom is not of this world. If My kingdom were of this world, My servants would fight, so that I should not be delivered to the Jews; but now My kingdom is not from here."

Jesus provided some clarity relevant to our investigation of God's perspective on the use of deadly force. He told Pilate His disciples actually would fight to protect Him and to prevent His arrest if His kingdom were of this world. Jesus was teaching that the kings of this earth legitimately formulate armies of soldiers and servants who will fight and kill to protect their king and the kingdom over which he rules. According to Luke 22:49 Jesus' disciples evidently desired to exercise that right to protect their King when they saw He was about to be taken into custody:

> 49) When those around Him saw what was going to happen, they said to Him, "Lord, shall we strike with the sword?"

The details of Jesus' arrest also confirm the truth we have already gleaned about the soldiers who served in 1st century Israel. There is a description of those who were in the arrest team in John 18:3,12. There was a detachment of troops and officers from the Jews that came to arrest Jesus while carrying lanterns, torches, and weapons. The Lord's response to the arrest team is very interesting and can be found in Matthew 26:55, Mark 14:48-49, and Luke 22:52-53. There is a common theme located in each of these renderings of Jesus' response. For example, Luke 22:52-53 states:

> 52) Then Jesus said to the chief priests, captains of the temple, and the elders who had come to Him, "Have you come out, as against a robber, with swords and clubs? 53) "When I was with you daily in the temple, you did not try to seize Me. But this is your hour, and the power of darkness."

There's a consistent accusation by Jesus against the Jews who led the arrest party in each of these passages. He desired an explanation for being treated as a robber they were seeking to arrest. The Greek word used here for "robber" is the same word used to describe the two criminals who were executed with Jesus in Matthew 27:38.(44)

Evidently the type of crime committed by the "robber" was deemed heinous enough to warrant the death penalty as its punishment. It appears Jesus was teaching that the soldiers who intended to take a robber into custody would be justified in brandishing weapons like swords and clubs. If they were justified to carry the weapons they would be found just as righteous in using them to affect the arrest especially if the robber resisted during the seizure. This principle is similar to the teaching we received from King David in 2 Samuel 23:1-7.

However, the issue was they were not arresting a robber or any other criminal. Jesus never showed any propensity toward the use of violence. In fact, these same people had heard Him teach in the past and didn't take Him into custody. Jesus was surprised they would come so heavily armed to arrest a person as peaceful and law abiding as Himself.

The Dispensation of Grace

Peter

We will now search Scripture located in the Dispensation of Grace for passages that articulate God's perspective on the use of deadly force. We'll begin with the passage located in Acts 10:1-48 which covers the events involving another Roman centurion named Cornelius. The author of the book of Acts, Luke, started the chapter by describing Cornelius in Acts 10:1-2:

> 1) There was a certain man in Caesarea called Cornelius, a centurion of what was called the Italian Regiment, 2) a devout man who feared God with all his household, who gave alms generously to the people, and prayed to God always.

Evidently Cornelius was much like the other centurion we studied in Luke 7 and Matthew 8. Although he was a Gentile

Roman soldier who had much command authority as a leader of a regiment, he had come to faith in God possibly as a result of his tour of duty in Israel. This faith had spread through his own home as well. Yet Cornelius was still yearning to know more about God, and his prayers were heard.

Peter was summoned by God Himself to go and meet with Cornelius. The Lord's motive for this mission was actually two-fold. He was teaching Peter it was time for the Gentiles, who was any one person or nation that was not Jewish, to hear the gospel of Jesus in order to move into a relationship with their Creator. At the same time, God was also answering Cornelius' prayers to know Him more intimately.

Peter had a hard time accepting that the God of Israel would actually want to express His love toward the Gentiles. Nevertheless, the Lord sent two of Cornelius' servants and another soldier to go and fetch Peter in order to bring him to the centurion. The apostle obeyed the Lord and traveled with the men back to Cornelius' house. Peter explained the gospel of Christ to him, providing Cornelius the opportunity to have a relationship with God through faith in Jesus Christ.

Cornelius, along with others, heard the word of God from Peter and believed in the Christ. They received the Holy Spirit and were eventually baptized. The other believing Jews who accompanied Peter were astonished when they witnessed the love of God being poured out to the Gentiles by indwelling them with His Spirit.

Cornelius was a soldier who was trained to kill and probably had killed sometime in his career in service to his country. The first point I want to make from this passage in Acts 10 is similar to the one in Luke 7. Just as Jesus didn't rebuke the centurion in regards to his profession as a soldier, Peter also said nothing about the matter.

Peter, an apostle who was commissioned by Christ Himself, never instructed or admonished this new believer in Christ to leave his profession. Cornelius had demonstrated his great love for God. He certainly would want to please the One who died on the cross and rose again for him. Cornelius, like all who are saved by believing in Jesus, can honor and please the Savior by living an obedient life. However, I believe the following fact is just as convincing that Cornelius' profession was honorable to the Lord.

Remember, Cornelius was a devout and just man who genuinely sought to know God. He spent time in prayer and paid alms seeking God's heart and approval. Notice in Acts 10:4c-6 what Cornelius was told by the visiting angel:

> 4c) "Your prayers and your alms have come up for a memorial before God. 5) "Now send men to Joppa, and seek Simon whose surname is Peter. 6) "He is lodging with Simon, a tanner, whose is by the sea. **He will tell you what you must do.**"(emphasis mine)

Cornelius later shared with Peter his encounter with the angel which is found in Acts 10:30-33:

> 30) So Cornelius said, "Four days ago I was fasting until this hour; and at the ninth hour I prayed in my house, and behold, a man stood before me in bright clothing, 31) "and said, 'Cornelius, your prayer has been heard, and your alms are remembered in the sight of God. 32) 'Send therefore to Joppa and call Simon here, whose surname is Peter. He is lodging in the house of Simon, a tanner, by the sea. When he comes, he will speak to you.' 33) "So I sent to you immediately and you have done well to come. Now therefore, we are all present

before God, **to hear all the things commanded you by God**."(emphasis mine)

The crucial observation from these verses is that God heard and answered Cornelius' prayer. I used the bold emphasis in the verses to stress that Cornelius' desire was being answered by Peter's arrival in his life. The apostle then explained the Gospel of Christ which was the revelation Cornelius needed to hear in order to know God in a more intimate way.

This is significant because we know that according to James 5:16b, "The effective, fervent prayer of a righteous man avails much." In contrast, if we live our lives in disobedience to God's word, then even our prayers are an abomination (Proverbs 28:9). A man's prayer may be hindered if he does not dwell with his wife in an understanding way and if he fails to honor her (1 Peter 3:7).

We then can assume that Cornelius' life was considered by God to be righteous since He answered the centurion's prayer. In addition, since Cornelius was a soldier in profession before he prayed, and Peter didn't direct this new believer in Christ to abandon his career, we can conclude Cornelius was able to honor God through his service as a soldier, even as a service to the Roman empire.

So far we have only studied Scripture that involves the use of deadly force by the children of Israel, God's chosen national people, or Gentiles and Jews who are believers in Christ. If we were to stop here a legitimate concern may develop that any use of deadly force by soldiers or law enforcement personnel who don't even believe God exists is sinful or immoral. In order to address this possible dilemma, we will re-visit a passage we've already investigated during our study of the righteous use of capital punishment by the governments of the world.

Paul

When we previously studied Romans 12:19-13:5 we discovered the Apostle Paul confirmed several things about the human governmental institution. Its establishment and authority is from God. Those who break the laws of the land resist their rulers and ultimately sin against God. The purpose of the authority is to bring terror on those who do evil and praise to those who do good. The government does not bear the sword in vain. The government has the authority to execute the death penalty on the individual who practices evil. This is why those who do evil should fear.

The exacting of penal sentences is considered a form of God's temporal wrath upon the criminals of the land. When justice is done it will provide stability in the land by punishing the rebels and detouring future acts of evil. This is considered a ministry of every government to its people for good which is a result of God's common grace. When the government has executed a convicted criminal, we can justifiably declare, "it is good."

Now that we have reviewed this passage, let's consider one of the main concepts taught to us about the government: *the government does not bear the sword in vain.* We know the sword is an instrument of killing and death. This is how we reached the conclusion the government has the authority to execute those who do evil in the land. However, was the Apostle Paul teaching that the government's authority to take life is limited to the death penalty?

The administration of capital punishment can take years or even decades in some cases. If this authority is limited to the death penalty, the capability to bring fear into the hearts of those who do evil may be significantly decreased. The citizens of any land will be less safe if their government doesn't provide a more immediate deadly consequence for those who carry out violence against them. I believe Paul was indeed teaching that the governing authorities have been ordained to use deadly force and kill any criminal or aggressor who brings violence upon its people.

We must consider the contemporary setting of the Roman government during Paul's life time. The authority of arresting rebels of the government was ordained to its military and other special units like the Emperor's Praetorian Guard. The soldiers of this time held an additional duty as peace officers who not only arrested criminal offenders but also maintained order during any uprising or breach of the peace. An excellent example of this concept is recorded in a passage from the book of Acts which we previously studied earlier in this book.

The Apostle Paul was back in Jerusalem during his third missionary journey in Acts 21. According to verse 27 some Jews from Asia saw Paul in the temple. They stirred up the people and snatched him out of their place of worship. Their intent for seizing Paul is described in Acts 21:31-33:

> 31) Now as they were seeking to kill him, news came to the commander of the garrison that all Jerusalem was in an uproar. 32) He immediately took soldiers and centurions, and ran down to them. And when they saw the commander and the soldiers, they stopped beating Paul. 33) Then the commander came near and took him, and commanded him to be bound with chains; and he asked who he was and what he had done.

According to verse 35 Paul was beaten so badly he had to be carried by the soldiers as they negotiated the stairs of the barracks. The soldiers had just saved Paul's life from the mob attempting to kill him. We also learn later that the commander, Claudius Lysias, wrote a letter to the Roman governor, Felix, and mentioned this very incident involving Paul in Acts 23:26-27:

> 26) Claudius Lysias, To the most excellent governor Felix: Greetings. 27) This man was seized by the Jews and was about to be killed by them. Coming with the troops I rescued him, having learned that he was a Roman.

Ananias arrived to see Governor Felix while being accompanied by elders and an orator named Tertullus and gave the same account of the event in Acts 24:5-7:

> 5) "For we have found this man a plague, a creator of dissension among all the Jews throughout the world, and a ringleader of the sect of the Nazarenes. 6) "He even tried to profane the temple, and we seized him, and wanted to judge him according to our law. 7) "But the commander Lysias came by and **with great violence** (emphasis mine) took him out of our hands."

The Biblical narrative doesn't specifically mention if any lives were lost during Paul's rescue. However, this particular police action evidently involved great violence. What would one expect? When you have an angry mob beating a person to death and the armed Roman soldiers arrive to establish peace, there is no doubt the Roman commander accomplished his objective by deploying violence to stop the assault.

The Apostle Paul's account and perspective of this incident is the most interesting of them all. In Acts 26 Paul was able to speak to King Agrippa and present his case that the charges against him were false. The apostle told the king of his personal commission from the risen Christ to go out and preach the gospel. He then stated in Acts 26:21-23:

> 21) "For these reasons the Jews seized me in the temple and tried to kill me. 22) "Therefore, **having obtained help from God** (emphasis mine), to this day I stand, witnessing both to small and great, saying no other things that those which the prophets and Moses said would come- 23) "that the Christ would suffer, that He would be the first to rise from the dead, and would proclaim light to the Jewish people and to the Gentiles."

As we interpret Paul's claim contextually his rescue can ultimately be accredited to God Himself. In other words, God saved him through the Roman soldiers as they performed their additional function as peace officers. They responded to the scene of the deadly assault on Paul and took violent action against the aggressors to deliver him from their hands.

The soldier's primary weapon during this time was the sword. It was to be used in the commission of his duties in fighting the enemy nations of Rome and during the arrest of those who were committing civil unrest in the land. One of the Lord's primary goals of human government is to bring fear into the hearts of those who do evil in the land. It makes perfect sense that the government's legitimate use of the sword extends to those who actually carry one. Of course this would encompass those in the military and police agencies.

The weapon of choice that is carried by the government representative, such as soldiers and peace officers, is not carried in vain. As a result, the reality of forfeiting your life while in the process of committing evil in the land becomes even more potentially imminent. That weapon can be righteously deployed by any field delegate while attempting to maintain the peace and provide security for the citizens of the land.

In addition, since he was speaking in context of the Roman government, I believe Paul was teaching that God's ministry through the ruling authorities is a universal principle. In other words, every nation in the world has the right to outfit a military and policing force in order to provide security and the protection of its sovereignty. Because of the evil of this present world there must be a deterrent to aggressive acts such as violent attacks by one nation upon another or one individual citizen upon another.

The criminals of the world must not be allowed to prowl without fear of imminent deadly consequences to their actions. I believe Paul was teaching that it would behoove the violator to fear instant serious bodily injury or death caused by those in authority if he chooses to rebel against the laws of the land. This reality will also provide the citizens with a greater sense of security while trusting their government to use deadly force upon domestic and foreign violent aggressors without delay.

Therefore, the purpose of the national or state military and police forces is to be that deterrent by providing the warning of lethal force against any entity that threatens security. The preventative aspect offered by our armed guardians is crucial and indispensable in maintaining order. One should attempt to envision the havoc evil men would reap on any particular society in which there is no such threat. There would be no danger of swift and severe retribution or death for their actions so they would be free to roam and destroy. My SWAT teammates and I once sported team shirts that bore on the back the following quote that is typically credited to George Orwell that conveys this concept:

"We sleep safe in our beds because rough men stand ready in the night to visit violence on those that would do us harm."

Yes, ladies, that also means you who are warriors and bear the sword for your community and country. Since God is very familiar with the concept conveyed in the above quote, He has designated the responsibility of protecting the people from such danger through the use of deadly force as a ministry of the human government. The people are not required to suffer through an act of violence, such as an active shooter, and hope only that the suspect runs out of ammunition or dies of natural causes. There are readily trained soldiers and police officers who will bring steel and lead to the scene with God's blessing to violently end the evil aggression being perpetrated upon their citizens.

When the people of any nation witness as their military goes to battle or when their policing authorities legally use deadly force in the commission of their duties, they can recognize that they are recipients of God's common grace that is dispensed to all nations regardless of their relational status with Him. That nation's inhabitants can legitimately say, "this is good!" Finally, I want to present Paul's affirmation of a principle that we did not cover earlier while we investigated Romans 13 and the government's authority in regards to the death penalty.

We have already witnessed the same idea taught by John the Baptist in Luke 3:14. John implied that the soldiers to whom he was speaking legitimately received pay for the fulfillment of their duties. This is a significant aspect of demonstrating the righteousness of the government's function in the use of deadly force including the administration of capital punishment. The Apostle Paul wrote the following in Romans 13:6:

6) For because of this you also pay taxes, for they are God's ministers attending continually to this very thing.

Paul again stressed the reality of the ministry provided by the government to the people of every nation. Similar to any other project or mission, funding is necessary for the accomplishment of the desired goals. The taxing system is the means through which we collect the required financial support for providing our ministers with salaries, equipment, and training. In 1 Corinthians 9:7 Paul iterated the same concept that our heroes who go to war or battle on our behalf should not do so at their own expense. We, the beneficiaries of their service, shall sustain the efforts of the government through our monetary contributions.

11

THE PEACEMAKER

I recently viewed an interesting episode of *Larry King Live* on *You Tube*. Mr. King was interviewing Dr. John MacArthur, Pastor of Grace Community Church in Sun Valley, California. The video clip was titled *"Christians Debate War, What Does the Bible Say About War?"* Mr. King asked Dr. MacArthur for the Biblical position on the legitimacy of war. Mr. MacArthur answered by quoting from Luke 14 and 22 and John 18. These are passages we previously investigated. Dr. MacArthur's biblically-based response was that there is indeed a noble time for war.

Mr. King then addressed another person on the Q&A panel, Bishop Melvin Talbert of the United Methodist Church. The Bishop strongly disagreed with Pastor MacArthur's answer and shared his own quote from the Scriptures. He first commented that Jesus preached like the prophets of the Old Testament in the books of Joel, Micah, and Isaiah. He said the message was for the nations to beat the swords into plowshares and the spears into pruning hooks. He concluded by claiming the Scriptures taught that the money from the wars would be invested in the children.(45)

With all due respect to Bishop Talbert, he actually misquoted the Scripture. The passages he apparently alluded to are in Isaiah

2:1-4 and Micah 4:1-4. Both of these passages of Scripture reveal events that shall occur in the time context of the future Millennial Kingdom. In other words, the prophet was not encouraging anyone to dismantle their weapons. The nations will turn their swords into plowshares and their spears into pruning hooks because they will be compelled by the ruling hand of Christ Himself. This shall occur during the period after Jesus returns and defeats the enemies of Israel at the end of the tribulation period. We will discuss that military victory more in the next chapter.

The only place in the book of Joel where this topic is mentioned is Joel 3:9-21. The time context of this passage is just prior to Jesus' return in which Christ will defeat those nations bearing down on Israel. The actual proclamation made to the nations at that time is an exact opposite of that quoted by the Bishop. The LORD will essentially call the nations to "prepare" for war. The following is found in Joel 3:9-11:

> 9) Proclaim this among the nations; "Prepare for war! Wake up the mighty men, Let all the men of war draw near, Let them come up.10) Beat your plowshares into swords and your pruning hooks into spears; Let the weak say, 'I am strong.'" 11) Assemble and come, all you nations, And gather together all around. Cause Your mighty ones to go down there, O LORD.

The purpose for this call to war prior to Messiah's rescue of Israel is found in Joel 3:17:

> 17) "So you shall know that I am the LORD your God, Dwelling in Zion My holy mountain. Then Jerusalem shall be holy, and no aliens shall ever pass through her again."

The Lord will call the Gentile nations to battle against the nation of Israel. The LORD will demonstrate His glory and power in the context of war. Sadly, because of the nature of our temporal world, the Lord's use of deadly force to save Israel will finally get the attention of Israel and the other global rulers who will ultimately bow to His rule.

I also encourage the study of another piece of the Hebrew Scripture in Jeremiah 51. The LORD God of Israel "raised up the spirit of the kings of the Medes" to go into Babylon and destroy the nation. This was to fulfill the vengeance of the LORD and the vengeance for His temple (Jeremiah 51:11). The Babylonians desecrated His temple during their initial invasion of the land of Judah and this was their punishment. According to Jeremiah 51:20 the LORD even called the armies of the Medes and Persians His "battle-ax and weapons of war" through whom He accomplished the following located in Jeremiah 51:24:

> 24) "And I will repay Babylon And all the inhabitants of Chaldea For all the evil they have done in Zion in your sight," says the LORD.

The Bishop also quoted a passage from the Sermon on the Mount. This particular sermon given by Jesus in the book of Matthew encompasses all of chapters 5-7. Bishop Talbert cited Matthew 5:9 where Jesus stated the following:

> 9) Blessed are the peacemakers, For they shall be called sons of God.

Without much inquiry of this section of Scripture one may conclude that the Bishop had made a persuasive argument. Jesus declared the one who makes peace is blessed and should be called a son of God. Most readers would automatically interpret the use of "peacemaker" as the complete opposite of taking up arms and using deadly force.

My key observation here is the word "peacemaker." The word is not "peacekeeper." The word "peacemaker" implies there is already hostility or violence between two or more parties. If this weren't so, then the better term would be "peacekeeper." That would require the act of preventing any hostility from starting between one or more parties during a time of already established peace. A peacemaker is one who chooses to enter into a volatile situation involving themselves or other parties in order to stop the aggression with peace as the intended result.

Of course, hostility exists at many different levels. The lowest level could begin with a disagreement leading to an argument and relational schism. The highest level would be the act of violence, such as the use of deadly force on another individual, group, or nation. There are indeed certain situations involving violent aggression that require the deployment of deadly force in order to re-establish safety and peace.

I am reminded of another scene from the movie *Rambo*, the same film I mentioned in Chapter Three. This scene is prior to Rambo's transport of the missionaries up the river from Thailand into Burma. Rambo was approached by the leader of the missionaries who identified himself as Michael Burnett. Michael offered compensation to Rambo if he would take his team into Burma.

Rambo immediately conveyed his opinion of the plan by describing Burma as a war zone. Michael responded by clarifying their mission was to provide medical support, medical attention, prayer books, and support to the Karen tribe's people. Michael added that they wanted to give support that will "help change peoples' lives."

> Rambo asked a very intriguing question in response to hearing their objectives. He asked Michael, "Are you bringing any weapons?"

> The missionary answered, "Of course not!"

> Rambo replied, "You're not changing anything."

We can interpret Rambo's comment to mean the people of Burma needed something more than what the missionary was offering. They needed a Peacemaker. The violence being brought against them was so overwhelming and the aggressors were so evil that talking was not an option. Even if there were no missionaries wanting to enter Burma to share Christ or bring other types of assistance, the people still needed to be saved physically from kidnap, torture, and murder.

In a roundabout way John Rambo was saying there is a time when immediate action is required and the administration of other assistance will just have to wait. The peacemaker, a man of war, would deploy into the hostile theater and rescue the Karen tribe's people by executing deadly force against their aggressor. Other types of aid would be safely implemented once the threat was subdued.

I am compelled to clarify the actual blessing of being called a "son of God" in Matthew 5:9. In my opinion, it seems to pertain to the believer in Christ who takes action as a peacemaker. I will write more on this later in the Conclusion of this book. I am presently responding to the pacifistic use of the word "peacemaker" by Bishop Talbert. I believe any person, believer or non-believer, can legitimately experience a sense of happiness and great accomplishment after establishing peace during a hostile situation. Whether that peace is obtained through the use of words or the legal use of deadly force, that person or group should be dubbed a peacemaker.

According to the Scriptures Israel will suffer an attack in the future of such hostility like the nation has never experienced in its history. The LORD's people will need a rescue from complete annihilation by the nations of the world. In the end Israel will indeed be delivered by the Lord Jesus at His return. We shall witness in the next chapter as King Jesus "makes His enemies His footstool" (Psalm 110:1-2). The Lord will reveal His divine and royal power as Israel's "Peacemaker," their Man of war.

12

JESUS THE MAN OF WAR

Dispensation of the Millennium

We are about to embark on a study of future events that are predicted or prophesied in the Scriptures. This is called Eschatology, the study of end times. The book of Revelation, written by the Apostle John, reveals the culmination of all things as we move into eternity. Although I didn't intend for this book to be an exhaustive study of end times, we need to invest some time on the subject in order to set the context for this section of our study.

There are diverse opinions of what the Scriptures teach about the end times. I believe they plainly teach what is known as the Pre-Tribulation/Pre-Millennial concept. In other words, I believe the Bible teaches the rapture of the church will occur prior to the seven-year tribulation period. The return of Christ will happen at the end of the tribulation period but prior to His 1,000 year reign here on earth.

We are presently living in the Dispensation of Grace. The next crucial event that will occur in regards to end times is what is called the "Rapture" when the church shall be "caught up" to be with the

Lord. Sometime after that the seven-year Tribulation period will begin. This seven-year period is believed by many scholars to be the 70th week from Daniel 9:25-27 in which God finally deals with the nation of Israel. This is also the period where the Anti-Christ will come into power and the world shall suffer through God's judgment like never before in history.

Although the seven-year tribulation period will involve the entire world, it culminates in the city of Jerusalem. The nations of the world shall be drawn into the area in order to take Jerusalem. Just as the city appears to be on the brink of destruction, Israel's messiah, Jesus Christ, will return with His church. The church is every person who has believed in Jesus Christ as Savior from Acts 2 until the Rapture. Christ will defeat Israel's enemies and set up His rule as the King of Israel. He shall rule and govern this present earth from Jerusalem for 1,000 years which is why it is dubbed the Millennial Kingdom.

For the purpose of our investigation we will focus our attention on the return of Christ which will occur at the end of the Tribulation Period. Interestingly, we find revelation on this subject in both the Hebrew Scriptures and the Newer Testament. The passages we will study are located in Ezekiel 39, Zechariah 12 and 14, and Revelation 19. The Hebrew Scriptures tell of the Messiah, the Anointed One, who will finally bring national salvation to Israel for which the Jewish people have been waiting throughout the ages.

Christians believe Jesus of Nazareth is the anticipated Jewish Messiah. We believe the Messiah had a first advent in which He came to earth as a man and paid for the sins of the world. Through faith in what God has accomplished through Jesus' atoning death, you and I may have a relationship with our Creator. Jesus was crucified on the cross, bodily rose from the dead, ascended into heaven, and is presently sitting at the right hand of the Father waiting to come back again (Psalm 110:1-2, Hebrews 10:12-13). The nation of Israel will see Him at His return and shall embrace Him as their Messiah (Zechariah 12: 9-10, Revelation 1:7).

Zechariah 12:3 states the following:

> 3) "And it shall happen in that day that I will make Jerusalem a very heavy stone for all peoples; all who would heave it away will surely be cut in pieces, though all nations of the earth are gathered against it.

Zechariah 12:8-9 states the following:

> 8) "In that day the LORD will defend the inhabitants of Jerusalem; the one who is feeble among them in that day shall be like David, and the house of David shall be like God, like the Angel of the LORD before them. 9) "It shall be in that day that I will seek to destroy all the nations that come against Jerusalem.

Zechariah 14:1-4 states the following:

> 1) Behold, the day of the LORD is coming, and your spoil will be divided in your midst. 2) For I will gather all the nations to battle against Jerusalem; the city shall be taken, the houses rifled, And the women ravished. Half of the city shall go into captivity, But the remnant of the people shall not be cut off from the city. 3) Then the LORD will go forth and fight against those nations, as He fights in the day of battle. 4) And in that day His feet will stand on the Mount of Olives, which faces Jerusalem on the east. And the Mount of Olives shall be split in two, from east to west, making a very large valley; Half of the mountain shall move toward the north and half of it toward the south.

Observe how Zechariah 14:4 states that the LORD has feet. This shall be fulfilled for the LORD shall stand on the Mount of Olives as the Man Jesus Christ, Who is God in flesh. This is precisely why I wondered if the Hebrew Scriptures that ascribe human like characteristics to God should be dubbed anthropomorphic. It's possible that since God is eternal He was revealing Scripture while already having in mind the incarnation of God the Son.

The nations will be poised to destroy Jerusalem at this point as the Tribulation period comes to an end. It appears the Mount of Olives will split in two when His feet hit the deck. Zechariah 14:8 describes living waters that will probably flow through this valley to the Dead Sea east of the city and to the Mediterranean Sea which is to the west. Ezekiel describes the same water that will regenerate the Dead Sea so that even fish will dwell in it. In fact, people will be fishing in the Dead Sea during the Millennial Kingdom according to Ezekiel 47:1-12.

The war that will to take place in the region is usually called the Battle of Armageddon or the Campaign of Armageddon. The Scriptures clearly indicate this battle will be the most ferocious and violent scene of combat ever recorded in the history of man. The theater will house more souls than any other campaign which is why the death toll and the carnage will also be in record proportions. Ezekiel provided some description to help us envision this in Ezekiel 39:12-20.

Ezekiel starts by revealing in verse 12 that Israel will be burying the dead for seven months. Then he continues through verse 15 describing how search parties shall be dispatched to find the dead and their remains for the purpose of cleansing the land. Markers will be left by the search party when a man's bone is found which will eventually be buried.

According to Ezekiel 39:17-20 the LORD instructed the prophet to call the birds of the air and the beast of the field to the scene. They are offered a sacrificial meal provided by the LORD Himself consisting of flesh to eat and blood to drink. The blood and flesh will be of the mighty men of war, princes, and other animals. Notice the instructions in Ezekiel 39:19-20:

> 19) You shall eat fat till you are full, and drink blood till you are drunk, at My sacrificial meal Which I am sacrificing for you. 20) You shall be filled at My table With horses and riders, With mighty men and with all the men of war," says the LORD GOD.

The picture Ezekiel painted for us is one of absolute carnage. Some Bible scholars believe the Apostle John described the same scene in Revelation 14:20:

> 20) And the winepress was trampled outside the city, and blood came out of the winepress, up to the horses' bridle, for one thousand six hundred furlongs.

John described a scene containing a quantity of shed blood rising up to a horse's bridle for almost 200 miles. I agree it's hard to imagine but we must consider the fact the armies of the east alone will consist of a group of 200,000,000 men. There shall be a colossal amount people involved in this massive and very violent battle which shall occur at the end of the tribulation period, culminating with the rescue of Jerusalem. Yet, the obvious million dollar question is: Who do the Scriptures indicate shall kill so many people during that rescue? The Apostle John provided the clue in Revelation 19:11-16:

> 11) Now I saw heaven opened, and behold, a white horse. And He who sat on him was called Faithful and True, and

in righteousness He judges and **makes war** (emphasis mine). 12) His eyes were like a flame of fire, and on His head were many crowns. He had a name written that no one knew except Himself. 13) He was clothed with a robe dipped in blood, and His name is called the Word of God. 14) And the armies of heaven, clothed in fine linen, white and clean, followed Him on white horses. 15) Now out of His mouth goes a sharp sword, that with it He should strike the nations. And He Himself will rule them with a rod of iron. He Himself treads the winepress of the fierceness and wrath of Almighty God. 16) And He has on His robe and on His thigh a name written:

KING OF KINGS AND LORD OF LORDS.

The million dollar question is answered. There's no doubt John was describing the Lord Jesus Himself. Notice all the descriptions of Him and His purposes. Clearly, Jesus will not come back as a lamb. He will return as the Lion of Judah and He will judge and make war. He will save the nation of Israel by fighting and killing her enemies. This will be Jesus the "Peacemaker" in action. He will establish peace out of the most chaotic and violent aggression ever witnessed by men. In my humble opinion, Jesus Christ is the One spoken of when Moses said in Exodus 15:3:

3) The LORD is a man of war; The LORD is His name.

The Apostle Paul further revealed in 1 Corinthians 10:1-4 that it was Christ Who ministered to Moses and Israel as they fled Egypt:

1) Moreover, brethren, I do not want you to be unaware that all our fathers were under the cloud, all passed through the sea, 2) all were baptized into Moses in the cloud and in the sea, 3) all ate the same spiritual food, 4) and all drank the same spiritual drink. For they drank

of that spiritual Rock that followed them, and that Rock was Christ.

It was the Spirit of Christ who revealed to Moses that the LORD is a Man of war. God's Holy Spirit experiences the eternal moment while we understand only the linear aspect of time. The ministry to Israel as their Peacemaker, their Man of war, was accomplished in their defeat of Egypt. By the same person the nation shall finally experience national salvation at the end of the Great Tribulation.

The carnage of Armageddon was also described by John in Revelation 19:17-18, which is very similar to the description given in Ezekiel 39. The apostle revealed what he saw during his vision in Revelation 19:17-18:

> 17) Then I saw an angel standing in the sun; and he cried with a loud voice, saying to all the birds that fly in the midst of heaven, "Come and gather together for the supper of the great God, 18) "That you may eat the flesh of kings, the flesh of captains, the flesh of mighty men, the flesh of horses and those who sit on them, and the flesh of the people, both small and great."

John again briefly described the details of the battle for us in Revelation 19:19,21:

> 19) And I saw the beast, the kings of the earth, and their armies, gathered together to make war against Him who sat on the horse and against His army.

> 21) And the rest were killed with the sword which proceeded from the mouth of Him who sat on the horse. And all the birds were filled with their flesh.

The prophet Zechariah also added the following to the scene of the great campaign of Armageddon in Zechariah 14:12:

> 12) And this shall be the plague with which the LORD will strike all the peoples who fought against Jerusalem: Their flesh shall dissolve while they stand on their feet, their eyes shall dissolve in their sockets, and their tongues shall dissolve in their mouths.

We have made the case from the Scriptures that Jesus Christ shall return to earth with great power and wrath for the nations who choose to fight against Him and His people Israel. However, there is a secondary purpose for Jesus' fierce rescue of the nation Israel.

It's important to remember Jesus shall immediately set up His rule and kingdom here on earth at His return. This takes us into the Lord's 1,000-year rule of the earth as Satan is cast into prison (Revelation 20:2-3). Jesus will reign over the kingdoms of earth while He remains in Jerusalem. Therefore, He'll return with the additional intention to rule and judge the nations. Let's revisit Revelation 19:15:

> 15) Now out of His mouth goes a sharp sword, that with it He should strike the nations. And He Himself will rule them with a rod of iron.

His reign as King will occur during what's often called the Millennial Kingdom. The nations who survive through the initial assault will have witnessed the power of Christ. His divine force and authority shall provide the nations incentive to yield to Him. For example, notice the description of this time period in Zechariah 14:16-17:

16) And it shall come to pass that everyone who is left of all the nations which came against Jerusalem shall go up from year to year to worship the King, The LORD of hosts and to keep the Feast of Tabernacles.17) And it shall be that whichever of the families of the earth do not come up to Jerusalem to worship the King, The LORD of hosts, on them there will be no rain.

Jesus will demand the worship He rightly deserves. There shall be a penalty inflicted on those who refuse to bow to Him: That area will receive no rain. The land will dry up and they will be without the life-preserving water. At first glance this may not seem like much of a punishment. We went through the worst drought in Texas history during the summer of 2011. It was very humbling to witness as our water levels diminished and the daily high temperature remained above 100 degrees for months straight.

We find the same kind of Messianic Millennial Kingdom warning to the kings of the earth in Psalm 2:7-12:

7) "I will declare the decree; The LORD has said to Me, 'You are My Son, Today I have begotten you. 8) Ask of Me, and I will give You the nations for Your inheritance, And the ends of the earth for Your possession. 9) You shall break them with a rod of iron; You shall dash them to pieces like a potter's vessel.'" 10) Now therefore, be wise, O kings; Be instructed, you judges of the earth. 11) Serve the LORD with fear and rejoice with trembling. 12) Kiss the Son, lest He be angry, And you perish in the way, When His wrath is kindled but a little. Blessed are all those who put their trust in Him.

The message is for the nations and peoples living during the millennial reign of the Son of God. It will behoove them to "kiss the Son" as a sign of worship. This is translated in the *New American Standard Bible* as "pay homage to the Son." There will no longer be the opportunity to mock God and refuse to worship Him without immediate consequences. Forever gone will be questions similar to those Asaph asked in Psalm 73 as he watched as the wicked prospered and mocked God by asking, "how does God know?" The warning to those who refuse to let Christ rule over them is very simple: Worship Him or you will experience His temporal wrath. The King of Kings and Lord of Lords will immediately punish those who rebel against Him.

It will be an awesome experience as one King governs and makes decisions for the entire earth. This future global rule shall be led by the God/Man, Jesus. The people will rest assured that all of His decisions and judgments are good and righteous. There will be no corruption in Him or in the methods of His reign. The Warrior King and Savior will finally reveal to the peoples of the earth the pleasure of living under the pure and just leadership of God Himself.

Satan will have been thrown into a prison while the millennial kingdom proceeds on this present earth. There will be true peace in the world while Christ Himself rules as King of Kings. He will finally fulfill Psalm 110:1-2 by "making His enemies His footstool." At the end of the millennium Satan will be released for a short period. Once he is freed the Devil shall deceive enough people to execute one more attack on Christ in Jerusalem. The coup will be defeated and Satan will be thrown into the Lake of Fire. The Great White Throne Judgment shall follow where all of its participants are also condemned to the Lake of Fire. These participants shall be every person throughout history who failed to take God at His word and believe in His Messiah, Jesus Christ.

The LORD shall destroy the heavens and the earth and replace them with the new heavens and the new earth, according to Revelation 21:1 and 2 Peter 3:10-13. The New Jerusalem will then come down out of heaven from God and every person who has ever lived will proceed into eternity either with Christ or without Him.

The Scripture is clear. Jesus Christ shall return as the Warrior King of Israel, their Man of war. He shall glorify Himself in the context of war where He will use deadly force and kill in order to save Israel from her enemies and establish His Kingdom. The truth of Jesus' future personal use of deadly force is compelling. It further demonstrates His practical perspective on deadly force which should encourage any Christian who may potentially kill or has killed in the contexts we have discussed in this book.

CONCLUSION

Jesus Christ's Perspective on Killing

Clearly we have established a good case for the intended meaning of Exodus 20:13. We located and studied an abundant amount of Scripture through all seven dispensations from Genesis to Revelation that teach there are indeed times in which God either commanded or justified intentional homicide. Those specific situations are the death penalty and the use of deadly force in war, policing, and self-defense. Therefore, to translate רָצַח (*ratsach*) in Exodus 20:13 as merely "kill" and interpret the intended meaning of the verse to be in regards to all homicide must be deemed illogical. The specific term "murder" or unjustified intentional homicide is definitely a more logical translation and interpretation.

We also established this Biblical perspective on killing is consistent. God cannot be dichotomized. In other words, it would be incorrect to declare there is a perspective of the God of the Older Testament and there is a different perspective of the God of the Newer Testament, particularly in reference to this topic. We have demonstrated Christ's perspective in this matter is universal and eternal. The LORD has not repented or changed His mind in regards to the subject of killing. His perspective on the death penalty and the use of deadly force in war, policing, and self-defense has remained the same throughout history.

I am hopeful this conclusion will provide comfort and confidence for the believer in Christ who wants to honor Him with their life. This hope is especially directed toward those Christians whose occupation is inherently more apt to lead them into situations requiring they kill another person. Those Christians who perform their civic duty as a jurist on a capital punishment case can also share in the same confidence if they are assigned the task of sentencing a condemned person to death. The Christian citizen who kills another person in the act of self-defense can be assured that his fellowship with the Lord is not hindered. In fact, all of the above who kill in these justified situations can experience intimacy with the Lord because they have trusted in His teaching on killing rather than being persuaded by the perspective of the unbelieving world.

Perhaps you don't believe Jesus of Nazareth is the Christ He claimed to be, yet you are curious of what He thinks about a life experience such as killing. I am so glad you joined me in this investigation. I hope this has opened your eyes to the practical perspective the Scriptures teach on this matter. Please keep in mind that even the unbeliever who serves in a position described in Romans 13 is still considered a servant or a minister to their people.

We must not confuse this servant or minister status as having gained "acceptance" before our Holy God. Remember the death penalty that was administered in the garden of Eden. Adam's sin resulted in death. Adam and Eve experienced spiritual death that day and they were sent from the presence of the LORD. This is death: relational separation from the Creator.

What's worse is this penalty or curse is passed on to every son or daughter of Adam. In other words, we all come into this world spiritually dead and relationally separated from God. We are then destined for eternal separation from Him or what is also described as the "second death" or hell if we experience physical death while still in that relational status. We are hopeless, inept to bridge this relational gap between God and ourselves. That is the bad news.

Do not fret. As I mentioned in Chapter 3 the main theme of the Bible is God's rescue or salvation of man from the penalty of death. The love God has for you and me is greater than any dilemma we could ever imagine. The Apostle Paul testified of this great love in Romans 5:6-8:

> 6) For when we were still without strength, in due time Christ died for the ungodly. 7) For scarcely for a righteous man will one die; yet perhaps for a good man someone would even dare to die. 8) But God demonstrates His own love toward us, in that while we were still sinners, Christ died for us.

God the Son came to earth and took on sinless humanity. He was born into this world and lived a sinless life. He alone was able to do this because He is the God-Man. He then allowed Himself to be crucified and He died on the cross for our sin. He paid in full the penalty demanded by our Holy God. He died for us, sinners. Romans 5:10 teaches that we were even enemies of God when He died for us. Jesus' bodily resurrection was proof that He is who He claimed to be and that God's justice has been satisfied.

The Scriptures are abundantly clear that we are saved by God's grace through faith (John 3:16 and Ephesians 2:8-9). If you will simply believe Jesus did that for you, you will have started your eternal life or eternal relationship with Him. For Jesus described eternal life in John 17:1b-3 as having a "relationship" with the

Father. While praying to His Father just prior to His arrest, Jesus said the following:

> 1b) "Father, the hour has come. Glorify Your Son, that Your Son also may glorify You, 2) "as You have given Him authority over all flesh, that He should give eternal life to as many as You have given Him. 3) "And this is eternal life, that they may **know You** (emphasis mine), the only true God, and Jesus Christ whom You have sent.

It is the Greek word γινώσκωσιν (*ginōskōsin*) that is translated to the English verb "know" in John 17:3. This term is used to express an experiential and relational knowledge of another.(46) Eternal life is not mere eternal existence. It is an eternal relationship with our God, bringing Him the glory, which is the purpose of our creation. I hope you will make that decision to believe in Him today. If you have believed in Him, cultivate that relationship through prayer and by listening to Him through the Scriptures. Find a local church that lives from the Bible so you may be fed the word of God.

Finally, I want to encourage you to test any conclusion claimed to be from an investigation of the Bible. Contextually examine the Scriptures with the goal of reaching the author's intended meaning. You shall protect yourself from the teachers of false doctrine and you will be on the road to spiritual maturity as declared in 2 Timothy 3:16-17, "All Scripture is given by inspiration of God, and is profitable for doctrine, for reproof, for correction, for instruction in righteousness, that the man of God may be complete, thoroughly equipped for every good work."

BIBLIOGRAPHY

1. Geisler, Norman. *Systematic Theology: Volume One, Introduction, Bible*. Bloomington: Bethany House Publishers, 2002, p. 240.

2. Biblos.com (http://interlinearbible.org/exodus/20-13.htm)

3. Biblos.com (http://interlinearbible.org/deuteronomy/5-17.htm)

4. Biblos.com (http://interlinearbible.org/genesis/4-8.htm)

5. Biblos.com (http://interlinearbible.org/genesis/4-15.htm)

6. Biblos.com (http://concordances.org/hebrew/strongs_2026.htm)

7. Biblos.com (http://concordances.org/hebrew/strongs_5221.htm)

8. Biblos.com (http://interlinearbible.org/deuteronomy/27.htm)

9. Biblos.com (http://concordances.org/hebrew/strongs_4191.htm)

10. Biblos.com (http://interlinearbible.org/genesis/37.htm)

11. Biblos.com (http://concordances.org/hebrew/strongs_8210.htm)

12. Biblos.com (http://concordances.org/hebrew/strongs_7819.htm)

13. Biblos.com (http://concordances.org/hebrew/strongs_2076.htm)

14. Biblos.com (http://concordances.org/hebrew/strongs_2874.htm)

15. Biblos.com (http://concordances.org/hebrew/strongs_2491.htm)

16. Biblos.com (http://concordances.org/hebrew/7523.htm)

17. Biblos.com (http://concordances.org/hebrew/veratzach_7523.htm)

18. Biblos.com (http://concordances.org/hebrew/harotzeach_7523.htm)

19. Biblos.com (http://concordances.org/greek/strongs_5407.htm)

20. Geisler, Norman. *Systematic Theology: Volume One, Introduction, Bible*. Bloomington: Bethany House Publishers, 2002, p.178-179.

21. Louw, J.P. *Semantics of New Testament Greek*. Philadelphia: Fortress; Chicago, CA: Scholars Press, 1982, p.40.

22. Barr, James. *The Semantics of Biblical Languages*. London: Oxford University Press, 1961, p.218.

23. *Blacks Law Dictionary: Deluxe Eighth Edition*. Bryan A. Garner, Editor in Chief. 2004, p.406.

24. *Blacks Law Dictionary: Deluxe Eighth Edition*. Bryan A. Garner, Editor in Chief. 2004, p.406-407.

25. *Blacks Law Dictionary: Deluxe Eighth Edition*. Bryan A. Garner, Editor in Chief. 2004, p.751.

26. *Texas Criminal and Traffic Law Manual, LexisNexis*: 2011-2012 Edition. Charlottesville, Matthew Bender and Company, 2011, p. 35-36.

27. *Texas Criminal and Traffic Law Manual, LexisNexis*: 2011-2012 Edition. Charlottesville, Matthew Bender and Company, 2011, p. 14.

28. *Texas Criminal and Traffic Law Manual, LexisNexis*: 2011-2012 Edition. Charlottesville, Matthew Bender and Company, 2011, p. 15.

29. Ryrie, Charles C. *Dispensation Today*. Chicago: Moody Press, 1965, p.31.

30. Ryrie, Charles C. *Dispensation Today*. Chicago: Moody Press, 1965, p.57-64.

31. Wikipedia. http://en.wikipedia.org/wiki/Karla_Faye_Tucker.

32. Ryrie, Charles C. *Ryrie Study Bible, Expanded Edition*: New American Standard. Chicago: Moody Press, 1995, p.141 (note on Ex. 31:14-15).

33. Ryrie, Charles C. *Ryrie Study Bible, Expanded Edition*: New American Standard. Chicago: Moody Press, 1995, p.1010.

34. Strobbel, Lee. *The Case For Christ*. Grand Rapids, Michigan: Zondervan Publishing House, 1998, p.197-198

35. Vine, W.E. *An Expository Dictionary of New Testament Words*. Old Tappan, New Jersey: Fleming H. Revell Company, 1940, Vol. 3, P. 72.

36. Vine, W.E. *An Expository Dictionary of New Testament Words*. Old Tappan, New Jersey: Fleming H. Revell Company, 1940, Vol. 1, P. 90.

37. Vine, W.E. *An Expository Dictionary of New Testament Words*. Old Tappan, New Jersey: Fleming H. Revell Company, 1940, Vol. 5, P. 184.

38. Biblos.com (http://concordances.org/greek/strongs_3709.htm)

39. *Texas Criminal and Traffic Law Manual, LexisNexis*: 2011-2012 Edition. Charlottesville, Matthew Bender and Company, 2011, p. 17-18.

40. Ryrie, Charles C. *Ryrie Study Bible, Expanded Edition*: New American Standard. Chicago: Moody Press, 1995, p.125.

41. The Nelson Study Bible: New King James Version, Second Edition. Nashville: Thomas Nelson Publishers, 2007, P126.

42. Wikipedia. (http://en.wikipedia.org/wiki/Alvin_C._York)

43. The Legacy Study Bible: New King James Version. Hank Hanegraff, General Editor. Nashville: Thomas Nelson Publishers, 2006, P.278.

44. Marshall, Alfred. *The NASB Interlinear Greek-English New Testament*. Grand Rapids: Zondervan Publishing House, 1984, P.130; 341.

45. Youtube. (http://www.youtube.com/watch?v=FLKya5kz5Uw)

46. Biblos.com (http://concordances.org/greek/1097.htm)

DEAR FRIEND:

T hank you for taking the time to read *Jesus Christ on Killing*. I pray you were enlightened and encouraged by it. My desire is you have discovered something new that has changed your view of our Savior, Jesus Christ. Perhaps you don't believe in Jesus as your Savior but this book has stirred your heart to investigate the Scriptures further. Maybe you are a devoted disciple of Christ but you were not aware of His view on killing. If either of these descriptions is true for you, then my goal was accomplished and I have provided some clarity on the topic of killing while emphasizing the authority of the Holy Bible.

It would bring me great joy if you contact us at the web site listed below and share your feedback regarding my book. We are considering producing a workbook as a supplemental tool for studying *Jesus Christ on Killing* as a resource for individual or group study. Your comments and questions are invaluable in creating an effective product. You can also order books for yourself, a friend, or a loved one on our web site. I also encourage you to contact me and let me know how I can pray for you.

Finally, I ask for your prayers, in which I am always in need. Also, please pray that my book will bring glory to God and move hearts to believe in His Son, Jesus Christ, as their Savior.

Blessings,
Sgt. Charlie Eipper

Contact us at www.jesuschristonkilling.com